Customer-Oriented Planning

ROBERT W. FERRELL

Customer-Oriented Planning

AMERICAN MANAGEMENT ASSOCIATION

Foreword

Businessmen attend few conferences today without hearing a speaker on some phase of planning. Most of the periodicals they read devote many pages to the subject annually. They see numerous books, and an ever-increasing assortment of job descriptions, with the word "planning" in their titles.

Much of the literature is addressed either to the necessity for planning, and planning theory generally, or to certain techniques applicable to such specialized areas of activity as market research, sales, finance, or R&D. Particularly, over the past decade, a great deal of effort has gone into explaining the theory of planning for the company as a whole in terms of a marketing concept. However, there is very little published material which even attempts to bridge the gap between this or any other theory and the actual practice of planning for the company as a whole. Practitioners and students have limited sources to which they can turn for information on basic, overall procedures. As the need for business planning is increasingly recognized, instinctively or not, it is correspondingly imperative that sound planning methods be developed. Otherwise, business planning will not only assume the character of a passing fad but will misdirect and stunt the profitable growth of many companies.

Such considerations prompt this book.

The writer does not presume to know all the answers to these questions of theory and procedures, much less offer them in the pages to follow. He does attempt to *suggest* the answers to the basic questions in hopes that he may thereby accelerate the progress of American business in developing and applying certain fundamental management concepts. These suggestions stem from more than 25 years of personal involvement and observation in a broad range of positions and fields of business activity—years which confirm the urgent necessity for a more professional, less opportunistic and improvised conduct of all business. We managers are too often guilty of what might be described—perhaps too accurately—as malpractice.

Sound practice can stem only from sound theory. Therefore, although this book is primarily directed toward the one rather than the other, the fundamental concepts which underlie or dictate the procedures outlined are identified and explained. It is hoped that this treatment will assist the reader in gaining a full understanding of the author's suggestions as to planning policy and procedures and, more important, in analyzing these suggestions critically as a means of developing improved theories and techniques. The fundamental concept which should direct the establishment and application of a business planning process with its related activities is the one here called *customer orientation*. This concept, explained at some length, is the underlying theme of every discussion. Like the others which are mentioned, it is not new in essence. However, the recommendations for the application and implementation of these concepts should suggest new meaning and enhance their significance.

What is said here applies in general to all kinds of businesses. Particular, and in some instances detailed, emphasis is laid on the role of the marketing function because of its importance and our current failure to understand fully this evolving area of specialization. If this emphasis appears to be an expression of one interpretation of the so-called marketing concept—or, more probably, an extension of that concept—it is merely a coincidence. This concept of customer orientation is intentionally not offered under a banner which might obscure its meaning or at least hinder its acceptance or rejection on the basis of its own merits.

Hopefully this book will offer food for thought to people both in and out of business circles, to admitted students and to professed practitioners of any and all business activities. This last group should find in it at least a few clues to the solution of some important practical, everyday business problems. For the guidance of those with special rather than general interests, the content may be summarized as follows:

> *Chapters 1-3* provide the foundation for the more detailed discussions and recommendations to follow. The three concepts fundamental to all subsequent suggestions are identified, and the sequential and functional elements of business planning are outlined separately.

In *Chapters 4-11* the sequential and functional elements of planning are blended and explained in more detail. Chapter 9 affords increased, and more specific, recognition of the crossover from planning to integration and measurement. Chapters 10 and 11 suggest formats for planning statements and criteria for evaluating the planning process.

Chapters 12-15 deal first with some of the major organization problems connected with business planning and then propose a basic procedure, involving all specialized areas, for the evaluation and control of research and engineering projects. The book ends with a list of criteria for evaluating the extent to which a business is customer-oriented and a look at the overall implications of customer-oriented planning for the individual in business.

—R. W. F.

Contents

PART ONE:

Fundamental Concepts

Most current attacks on costs are specialized and, therefore, relatively superficial. They can be made more meaningful as part of a basic, productive business-as-a-whole campaign. Pricing, at the same time, suffers from a debilitating cost-plus attitude which must be purged. Guides to the direction of this twin offensive are to be found in a rediscovery and more explicit implementation of three fundamentals underlying American business operations: (1) the relation of the business as a whole to its parts, (2) the crux of business success, and (3) the companion concept of customer orientation.

1. Orientation and Operation Of the Business as a Whole

FROM ITS INCEPTION, BUSINESS HAS BEEN CONFRONTED with the conflict between cost and price. Whether in simple or sophisticated form, business will continue to have this problem—whose other face is opportunity. The first step for American business is to welcome this problem, with all its new and increasing complexities, as its very own.

Most experienced businessmen will promptly respond to this suggestion by saying, "We do accept this cost-price problem as a matter of course. We could not stay in business, even for a matter of months, without that basic philosophy." But is this really true? Or is it only superficially true with respect to some obvious but relatively insignificant aspects of business and false concerning some less obvious but more fundamental and important facets of business life?

The Attack on Costs

Within the past quarter-century expenditures by American business for *research and development*—on its own initiative and under the sponsorship of government—have increased at a fantastic pace. Some estimates indicate that total costs in this area now exceed $15 billion a year[1]—with still more planned for the future. This enormous figure has been a source of national and individual company pride; some financial analysts have even used R&D expenditures as a basic indicator of investment preference. True, the caliber of research and development has substantially improved along with the expansion in effort. But if, by any standard, the increased expenditures do generate a reasonable amount of new information, products, and processes, is the cost to individual businesses commensurate with the possible payoff to those companies? If not, these expenditures should be viewed with alarm rather than with pride and complacency.[2]

American mass-production concepts and techniques are envied and imitated throughout the world. With continued progress toward automation, *manufacturing cost*, as such, is increasingly under control. However, with the loss of flexibility inherent in highly mechanized manufacturing, the total cost risk to business is multiplied many times. What formerly may have been expensive errors in product selection, timing of production, or even facilities planning now may assume the proportions of a catastrophe as the promise of substantial reductions in manufacturing cost turns quickly into the nightmare of bankruptcy.

Most businesses in the United States today are organized and staffed to do a professional job of *purchasing* the materials and supplies required for their operations. With the further development and broad application of such techniques as value analysis, even greater savings will be realized in the important cost areas for which purchasing people are responsible. However, their contribution to the control of costs is basically limited by the direction they receive concerning the kinds of things which should be purchased—and when. If a company is making and trying to sell a product which is "wrong" for its market, the best purchasing activity will only slightly minimize the total of all direct and indirect expenses so wastefully incurred.

[1] "Reviews of Data on Research and Development," 12th Annual Survey of the National Science Foundation, No. 41 NSF 63-40, September 1963.
[2] See Peter F. Drucker, "Twelve Fables of Research Management," *Harvard Business Review*, January-February 1963, pp. 103-108.

American business has also made progress in controlling and minimizing costs in the *financial area*. However, clever methods of providing capital for new ventures will only encourage increased costs, or even substantial losses, if such ventures are inappropriate to the company. Voluminous cost and other data can of course be obtained with incredible ease and speed, and still greater speed is anticipated with the installation of more and more sophisticated data-processing equipment and communication systems. But the possible savings to be derived from these systems are insignificant in comparison with the losses which can be incurred if the wrong data are processed and used or if the right data are misused in making decisions.

It is frequently pointed out that American business's biggest cost challenges and opportunities are in the area of *distribution*. This is obvious when advertising alone involves, as it does, a total expenditure in the neighborhood of $13 billion a year.[3] Any progress made by way of increasing productivity in sales, advertising, and other distribution activities cannot, however, offset to any appreciable extent the increased costs which can result from the distribution of wrong products, wrong services, or right products and right services at the wrong time or place.

Most employers in this country have recognized the necessity for an organized approach to *employee relations*. Some very sophisticated techniques have been developed in this field of management activity. Undoubtedly more are to come. However, one cannot but wonder whether they are leading to more or less control over this major cost area and, still more important, question whether they are building incentives for greater or less individual productivity.

All these attacks on cost are necessary and worthwhile. But they are not enough. They do not come to grips with the core problem—the cost of a business enterprise as a whole (the term "cost" being used in its broadest, not its strict accounting, sense). To repeat: Dire possibilities of increased costs or substantial losses are inherent in the segmented approach to cost control since each attack assumes the perspective of the special activity under consideration—as it should and must.

Manufacturing must concentrate on production problems. Engi-

[3] *Printers' Ink*, January 31, 1964, p. 5.

neering must be preoccupied with technology. Sales must focus on getting the order. Each must develop the greatest possible cost control and productivity within its area of specialization. However, the success of any business enterprise depends upon how these areas of specialization are synthesized—not only as to their cost but as to their combined results. The cost to the business as a whole, with its accompanying gain or loss, will be greater than the mere sum of the gain or loss within each separate area. Therefore, by far the most important attack on costs which can be launched by American business is from the perspective of *general management.*

If the statements of many business leaders today are to be taken at their face value, such an offensive is already under way. Chief executive officers and general managers throughout the country are personally worrying about costs. They are instituting special cost reduction campaigns, cutting advertising and research budgets, reorganizing to eliminate unnecessary personnel, giving up company planes and other "frills," supervising telephone and miscellaneous expense more closely. General management in some cases is even disposing of certain ventures which have not recently been profitable. Yet such action does not necessarily fill the prescription. It should be routine—it by no means represents an offensive of the kind that is needed. What more, then, is called for?

Pricing: Basic Management Attitudes

Before exploring the possibility of a different attack on costs by general management, it may be helpful to take a brief look at the present situation of American business with respect to prices.

American business, with few exceptions, has historically favored cost-plus pricing. This attitude has been nurtured by the Federal Government. In its wartime procurement, many contracts were expressly placed on a cost-plus-fee basis, and the fees were directly or indirectly related to the cost. Other contracts supposedly provided for a fixed price, but soon even these—thanks to the operation of renegotiation procedures—appeared in business's eyes to be modified cost-plus arrangements and were treated as such. And many of today's top management people either won their spurs or received their first training in business during that wartime period.

The Federal Government continues to this day to exert this influence through its procurement role—particularly, of course, in the defense industries—although improvements have been made in certain practices. Moreover, in roles other than that of a customer the Government likewise encourages a cost-plus approach to pricing. This may be seen in its attitude toward and, in some cases, its active participation in the settlement of strikes and threatened strikes. Even the legislative branch of the Federal Government, over the years, has leaned in this direction.

Another contributing factor has been the basic economic climate in which American business, for the most part, has been operating. With some license it can be said that, in the main, we have faced urgent if not seemingly unlimited demand. There has been more than enough to go around. Most competent and aggressive businesses, in most industries, have enjoyed increased sales yearly; from a volume standpoint, their principal problem has been to get their "proper" share of the increased volume available. So for many years, in keeping with a cost-plus philosophy, increased cost has been automatically built into price without seriously jeopardizing volume.

In the past few years the rate of profit as a percentage of sales has of course declined. This developing condition, though masked somewhat by total dollar profits, reflects among other things the increasing inability of business to pass higher costs on to the consumer. And, with the advent of competent foreign competition, the slackening of demand in some markets, and the persistence of "soft spots" in certain areas of the economy, it is becoming obvious to more and more segments of business that pricing from a cost-plus stance will not work. This lesson the department stores have been learning the hard way through their experiences with discounters.

Any change in basic attitudes toward pricing must come from general management, whatever special functions participate in its administration. It is, therefore, up to general management to provide a different approach to pricing as well as to cost control. A twin offensive is overdue. Fortunately, but not at all surprisingly, this twin offensive can and should involve more common than divergent efforts. Solutions to problems in both areas can draw upon the same sources—which can be rediscovered by a re-evaluation of some fundamental concepts and principles that we tend to lose sight of in our preoccupation with specialization, refinements in particular techniques, and even gimmicks. As Peter G. Peterson, president, Bell and Howell Company, has said:

> We need to replace some of our share-of-market "gadgeteering" with more conceptual thinking . . . thinking that looks at the changing of human wants and bridges these with the technical possibilities of the research and development revolution.

> We need conceptual minds that can help management with a vision of what our businesses could be . . . not what our businesses have been. Conventional marketing wisdom is not enough.[4]

Marketing Concept and Marketing Function

Over the past ten years a new specialization has been gaining at least lip service in business circles. It is called *the marketing function*. To some it is simply sales with a new name and image and is practiced as such. To others it is truly something new, but they cannot decide exactly what. They too practice it accordingly.

Some of the confusion is due to semantics. The term "marketing" is used, for example, to describe a functional area in business paralleling those of engineering, manufacturing, research, and finance. For simplification that is the *only* way the term is used in this book. However, "marketing" is also used to describe an attitude, philosophy, or orientation of a business. The desired orientation, to every business enterprise, can be more meaningfully and clearly described by the term "customer orientation." As will be explained, customer orientation depends heavily upon full performance of the marketing function, but it also requires the participation and unique contributions of all other company areas and of general management. This book attempts to explain the marketing function—like the other functional areas of specialization—in terms of the business, rather than explain the business in terms of the marketing function, in the hope that this approach will cut through the confusion and not simply add to it.

"Is the marketing concept yesterday's fad?" In answer to this question *Printers' Ink* suggests: "Not much has been heard about it lately. But as far as a practical business concept goes, it is as valid as

[4] "Conventional Wisdom and the Sixties," *Journal of Marketing*, April 1962, pp. 65-67.

ever. Maybe now that people have stopped talking about it, they'll really begin practicing it."[5] The trouble lies in the uncertainties which still surround the subject. Gerald E. Fisch, managing director of Payne-Ross, Limited, Montreal, summed it up when he told the Forty-Fifth National Conference of the American Marketing Association in June 1962: "I suspect not even three people in this room could agree precisely as to what it is, and how it should be applied."

Such new specializations—corporate planning is another—will each contribute something to improved business operations. Their influence may even be substantial as they mature in concept and practice. However, the solution to the basic problems of American business does not lie solely or even primarily in any one of them, any more than it does in the older company functions.

The General Management Challenge

No business enterprise is interested in research or engineering merely for the sake of research or engineering, regardless of the technical content of the product or service offered. Even firms which offer only consulting research or engineering services must direct them toward some end other than the abstract advancement or glorification of those disciplines. This is true of any specialized function or activity, whether it is of a manufacturing, financial, sales, personnel, or marketing nature.

All these activities can be justified only to the extent that they are required by the business as a whole, and its needs must determine the method by which they are performed. The efficiency and cost of performing them will depend upon skill and practice within each area of specialization, but even more upon skill and practice in blending them. The latter is the responsibility of general management. The extent to which this challenge is met in any business determines the extent to which the true potential of management— and of the business—will be realized.

Every business should be greater than the sum of its parts! Gerald A. Busch, vice president and director of marketing, Lockheed Propulsion Company, draws the following analogy from the field of science:

[5] Issue of January 4, 1963.

When our scientists split the atom, they find inside the nucleus of the atom and, swinging around it, electrons and other particles. You cannot see them, you cannot feel them, you cannot smell them, you cannot touch them. And yet the atom and its constituents are possessed of such great power that they constitute the building blocks of nature. So small a particle, the atom is yet able to contain so much power that out of it comes the hydrogen bomb. And why can such little things create such a great power? The answer is that by themselves, they are absolutely unimportant, absolutely unproductive. The power of these particles comes in their cooperation one with another, when put together in a planned way so as to result in a chain reaction. Then, despite the infinitesimal size of each particle, together they release so much energy as to offer the potential of controlling nations.[6]

And James W. Culliton, dean of the College of Foreign and Domestic Commerce, University of Notre Dame, suggests:

We are surrounded by evidence that mankind is in transition from one era of human thought and action to another—from what might be called the "Age of Analysis" to the "Age of Synthesis." Businessmen, being men of action, may well say: "So what?" But I submit that the change will exert—indeed, is already exerting—great pressures on practical decision making in the world of business, and that those who recognize and understand its meaning will be better equipped to benefit from the opportunities it opens up. . . .

The concept of the consumer-oriented company in a free economy, when it is actually applied, begins to make untenable the old kind of departmentalization in a business. A sales department which peddles what is made, a manufacturing department which makes what is easiest or cheapest, an engineering department that designs what it likes—these factors cannot be brought into line by some vague or even well-developed concept of coordination or organization of parts like building blocks; they cannot easily be arranged in a "summed-up" whole. As soon as the customer *really* becomes the focal point, every department has to be aware of him. The whole is *not* the sum of a good sales department, a good production department, a good engineering department, a good public relations department, and good other departments. Rather, the whole is the consumer-oriented business, and *it will be more or less healthy as it has parts which, in interrelationships with each other, work for or against the whole.*[7]

[6] "Management Action; A Case Study in Profit Therapy," in *Marketing Precision and Executive Action*, Charles H. Hindersman, editor, American Marketing Association, Chicago, Illinois, 1962, p. 90.
[7] "Age of Synthesis," *Harvard Business Review*, September-October 1962, p. 36.

This concept of wholeness as opposed to departmentalization is the first fundamental to which American business must return with new understanding. Others emerge when we try to answer the questions: Greater in what sense? What difference does it make, anyway, to the business enterprise? Or to the people in the enterprise? Or to its customers, its stockholders, the public, or government? How does general management achieve this goal? Who helps general management, when, and how?

Need for a Systems Approach

What we have said thus far amounts to this: The potential of a business, and its progress toward that potential, can be fully appreciated only in terms of its totality. Similarly, any organizational part of a business enterprise, and any particular business activity, can be best understood from the standpoint of expected contribution to the business as a whole. Seymour Tilles, recognizing the basic problem, proposes what he calls a "systems approach" to management.

> . . . Too many managers are thinking of themselves and of their companies in buggy-whip terms. They have a concept of management which rests on a point of view that has remained largely unchanged since it was formulated by Henri Fayol just after World War I. In the meantime, however, a deluge of important new ideas has swept across the business scene. Whole new fields of critical importance to management have emerged: cybernetics, integrated data processing, systems engineering, and a variety of others ranging from social psychology to Bayesian statistics. The impact of all these new ideas on management has been so fundamental that new ways of thinking about the manager's job are long overdue.
>
> The modern manager needs a new approach to his job for three reasons:
>
> 1. He must have a way of thinking about management that permits him to take account of the tremendous amount of new knowledge that is appearing.
>
> 2. He has to have a framework that permits him to relate one specialty with another in his work.
>
> 3. He must be able to raise his sights above the hurly-burly of

current in-company operations and understand how his company relates to its complex environment—to the other great systems of which it is a part.[8]

Ray R. Eppert, president, Burroughs Corporation, suggests that a business can be described in terms of a funnel.

The big end . . . of this corporate funnel, into which everything must be poured, is the production part of the company. The small end, or spout, out of which the total corporate effort must flow, is the marketing organization.

Into the wide mouth of this corporate funnel are poured research, design, engineering, planning, materials, labor, special skills, executive abilities, capital—everything necessary to produce the end products. The results of these resources—the end products—can only come out of the small end of the funnel; i.e., the *marketing activity*.

There are two very basic things to remember about a funnel. In the first place, it is the output of the small end of the funnel which determines how fast we can pour into the big end. If the input is faster than the output, the overflow—the excess goods inventory— spills onto the floor and runs to waste.

The second thing about a funnel is that its whole function is to direct the flow accurately, and this function is fulfilled only by the small end, which in this analogy means marketing.

The small end would be useless without the big end, but in the final analysis it is the small end which makes the whole funnel useful. *The prime objective should be to increase the capacity of the small end of the corporate funnel, thus permitting expansion of the input and the attainment of corporate growth.*[9]

Wroe Alderson, who over a number of years has urged the acceptance of the systems viewpoint and approach, has this to say about it in relation to the marketing concept:

Marketing men come to see the business firm as an operating system, to analyze it in terms of its inputs and outputs, to understand its destiny as an organic and growing entity in its marketing environment. The application of systems analysis to business activities is the common element of contemporary developments in marketing counsel, opera-

[8] "The Manager's Job: A Systems Approach," *Harvard Business Review*, January-February 1963, pp. 73-81.
[9] Speech before the American Marketing Association, June 1962.

tions research, and cost accounting. . . . The market analyst, the operations researcher, and the cost accountant can perform their services to management with greater insight by adopting this systems perspective. . . .[10]

This book not only recommends what might be called a systems approach but attempts to describe in broad outline, and in some instances to spell out in detail, the system that should be recognized and the way in which it should be operated.

Planning and What It Involves

Any system, or basic approach, is governed by some core thought or concept, and the dominant theme of any business can be summed up by our phrase "customer orientation." Easy to say and difficult to attain, it cannot become a reality if its many implications as to thought, action, and results are not fully appreciated. These implications and their significance begin to emerge from an examination of one of the most fundamental business activities: planning. The main vehicle for our discussion is, therefore, planning. Activities which precede or follow it are mentioned as they may be required to explain planning and to develop more fully the true meaning of customer orientation.

As early as 1957, Bruce Payne observed that "much of the work that goes on under the name of 'long-range planning' does not deserve the title at all. True long-range planning is still rare, and it involves a unique set of activities."[11] The lack of understanding of what is involved in top management planning is finally being admitted openly and is receiving the attention of people in academic and business circles alike.

Any exploration of the subject must of course start with the question, "What is the role, or purpose, of business in our society?" This query has inspired numerous philosophical discourses, many of which are stimulating and revealing. However, they mean little to the average businessman grappling with the hard, everyday realities of existence in his own particular activity. To him, the question is

[10] Alderson Associates, Inc., "Cost and Profit Outlook," January 1960.
[11] *Harvard Business Review*, March-April 1957, pp. 95-106.

theoretical, with no practical value. He is entirely willing to leave it to the elder statesmen in the business world, to the academicians, or even the politicians. This is a mistake for many reasons. From the purely selfish standpoint it is a mistake because in the answer to this question, at least insofar as it concerns the individual enterprise, are to be found our most truly basic principles of management planning and control.

What is the answer, from this standpoint, in its most pragmatic terms? What is the purpose of any particular business? To be success-ful! But the simplicity of this answer is deceptive and misleading. *When* is a business successful? When it increases its sales or services? When it increases profit as a percentage of sales or increases its re-turn on investment? When it improves its market position or its rate of product innovation?

There are any number of methods for measuring success, includ-ing very sophisticated techniques which supposedly provide, and are used to find, the right answer. They undoubtedly shed some light on the subject, but do they give the full answer? They do not if, as most of them do, they fail to reflect an understanding of the true nature of business success.

A Matter of Balance

What, in short, is the true nature of success for a business enter-prise in our country, whether it be big or small, concerned with making and selling a product or providing a service?

The success of any business is measured by the extent to which the resources of that business are kept in profitable growth balance with the customer needs served by those resources. This fundamental con-cept, with its many implications, is germane to all the thinking and suggestions which follow. It can be depicted as shown in Chart I—pro-vided we mentally project into the picture the inherent dynamics which this "still shot" does not reveal.

The block on the right, labeled "customer needs," covers a wide range from the spiritual to the materialistic. We all have needs; our awareness of them varies with time and circumstances, as most cer-tainly do the means with which—as individuals and as social, business, and political groups—we seek to satisfy them. No business can hope to serve all these needs or even any appreciable part of them. Every business, in order to survive, must serve some of them. Which? Every business, in its inception and until its demise, faces this persistent core question.

CHART I

THE CONCEPT OF BALANCE

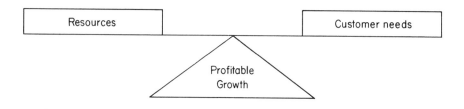

A basic factor in determining this answer is the particular capabilities of the business. These capabilities depend upon the resources available to it. What do we mean by "resources"? As used here, the term assumes the broadest possible interpretation so as to include such tangible items as manpower and factory facilities and such intangibles as know-how and reputation. The block on the left of Chart I represents the resources which are being used to meet the customer needs on the right.

Everyone associated with the enterprise—management, employees, owners—can enjoy the sweet smell of success when a profitable growth balance between customer needs and resources is achieved. Even when arrived at, however, this balance is not easily maintained. The customer-needs block is subject to constant direct attack by competitors seeking to serve these same needs by similar or different means. It is also modified by indirect competition—economic, social, and political influences which affect and sometimes diminish specific needs. Meanwhile, the resources block is going through changes of its own which, unless carefully managed, are not related to those connected with customer needs. All resources will deteriorate unless consciously preserved. Many will automatically generate others, which may turn into liabilities if their development is left undirected or if they are not applied satisfactorily.

Thus, with or without volition or action on the part of management, the profitable growth balance of the business is forever changing. This dynamic situation challenges the very survival of the business. However, inherent in this challenge is the life-giving incentive of our American system—the possibility of continuing, increasing profits for the company which sees its opportunities in terms of customer needs and pursues those opportunities to the satisfaction of the customer.

The Choice Today

Management's choice is very simple. It can, of course, let nature take its course. In this event it is only a matter of time before the customer-needs block erodes as competitors move in to offer improved service and the resources block gets out of proportion—whether through depleted resources that are not replaced or newly generated resources that are not fully utilized. Or management can try to be master of its own destiny, to some extent, through optimum use of the available resources to serve specific needs.

Although the choice is so elementary as often to be made unconsciously, the consequences are complex. The dire results of the first alternative are too obvious to require further comment. History is replete with examples; according to reports, the rate of business failures is mounting, and that trend is expected to continue in the near future. However, even the most conscious and deliberate decision to follow the second alternative is no guarantee of future success. It merely fixes management's stance on the first tee. The traps still facing the business, internal and external, are growing in number and complexity daily.

It is the typical, not the exceptional, company president who today asks the question: "What will be the major problem facing my business five years from now?" and answers it along these lines:

It will be the same problem, with greater dimensions and differing facets, as confronts us now—how to increase or at least maintain profits in spite of such adverse environmental factors as

1. More and different kinds of customers, in different locations, with increasingly discriminating demands concerning products and services.
2. Accelerated product obsolescence resulting from large research and development expenditures in the past and anticipated future increases in this area on the part of competitors, customers, and others.
3. Increasingly proficient means of serving customers other than the one that has been the historical foundation of my business's profitable growth.
4. Stronger domestic and foreign competition offering the same kinds of products as my business.
5. Stronger domestic and foreign competition offering different kinds of products which are equally acceptable—and, in some instances, more acceptable—to our customers in the service of their needs.
6. More dynamic changes in the nature, breadth, segmentation, and stratification of markets, at home and abroad.
7. Mounting depressants on profits due to constantly increasing costs as well as more aggressive competition.
8. More complex and demanding relationships with customers and competitors resulting from increasingly sophisticated management practices.

In broad outline, this president's problem—and that of most, if not all, other heads of business—is clear, now and for the future. In detail and in solution, it is more obscure and complicated. It also promises to become more so with the development of these and other trends.

To a businessman so beleaguered, can this simple concept of success be of any interest or practical use? It can and should be—if it serves as the cornerstone around which to develop or revitalize principles and procedures which have very specific application to immediate and long-range operating problems. First of all, it should remind management of the obvious but too often forgotten fact that no matter how well a business may perform any activity, no matter what resources it may possess, it cannot in any sense succeed or even survive if it does not know what particular customer needs it is capable of serving and gear the development, preservation, and full utilization of its resources to that service.

Is not this the real meaning of the term "customer orientation"? It certainly should be more than a catch phrase, more than an excuse for sales personnel to lavish entertainment on customers or even a rationale for prompter deliveries and better service in general. Certainly, too, it implies a directive to more people in the business than those having immediate contact with customers.

Customer orientation should be a way of business life—a state of being common to the business as a whole.[12] More specifically, this fundamental can be stated as follows: *Customer orientation is the awareness of and fulfillment of the concept that a business enterprise's profitable growth depends upon its future ability to serve selected customer needs rather than to sell particular products or services.*

Toward a Better Planning Sequence

Who does what to make customer orientation a way of business life? First, since general management always establishes the general policies of a business and the atmosphere in which it functions, general management must understand and accept the need for customer orientation and—through formal statements by managers at every company level—communicate to all concerned that this is the intended way. Further, since wishing will not make it so, general management must act, and get others to act, in a manner designed to make the concept a reality.

Management responsibility and action are often described in terms of planning, organizing, integrating (or coordinating), and measuring (or controlling). Among these, planning is paramount. It is important not only for its own sake but because it provides the only sound basis for organizing, integrating, and measuring.

In 1959 Peter F. Drucker raised the question, "What are the re-

[12] See Theodore Levitt, *Innovation in Marketing*, McGraw-Hill Book Company, New York, 1962. Mr. Levitt develops the basic necessity for customer orientation both fully and clearly.

quirements of this thing called long-range planning?" He then defined it generally in these terms:

> It is the continuous process of making *present entrepreneurial (risk taking) decisions* systematically and with the best possible knowledge of their futurity, organizing systematically *the efforts* needed to carry out these decisions, and measuring the results of these decisions against the expectations through *organized, systematic feedback.*[13]

Mr. Drucker then suggested that eight elements are involved in any long-range planning process: (1) objectives, which he recognized was an undefined and elusive term; (2) assumptions, what people believe to be true of the internal and external environment of the business; (3) expectations, likely future events or results; (4) alternative courses of action; (5) decisions; (6) decision structure; (7) impact stage, the reaction in all areas to action taken on a decision; and (8) actual results. Mr. Drucker said further, "We need an integrated decision structure for the business as a whole." In elaborating on this point he observed:

> We obviously also need for long-range planning managerial knowledge—knowledge with respect to the operations of a business. We need such knowledge as that of the resources available, especially the human resources, their capacities and their limitations. We need to know how to "translate" from business needs, business results, and business decisions into functional capacity and specialized effort. There is, after all, no functional decision, there is not even functional data, just as there is no functional profit, no functional loss, no functional investment, no functional risk, no functional customer, no functional product, and no functional image of a company. There is only a unified company product, risk investment and so on, hence only company performance and company results. Yet at the same time the work obviously has to be done by people each of whom has to be specialized. Hence for a decision to be possible, we must be able to integrate divergent individual knowledges and capacities into one organization potential; and for a decision to be effective, we must be able to translate it into a diversity of individual and expert, yet focused, efforts.

It would appear, from the standpoint of the major problems in operating a business as seen by thoughtful students and practitioners,

[13] "Long-Range Planning," *Management Science,* Vol. 5, No. 3, April 1959.

and in view of the three fundamentals which we have previously identified, that

- Planning must be done for the business as a whole;
- Planning must be directed toward achieving a profitable growth balance between customer needs and resources; and
- Planning must assist in the customer orientation of the business.

Is this conclusion correct? And, if it is, how do we do such planning? As a first step in answering this broad question, it is helpful to pose the following assumption and attempt to answer the specific query implied. There should be some sequence for planning which is more proficient than others. What is it?

As will be pointed out in later chapters, it is more accurate and meaningful to consider all planning as continuous and resembling a circle. However, a certain perspective is provided by examining the elements of planning in a straight line with a supposed beginning and end. When these elements and their sequence are fixed with some certainty and detail relative to planning for the business as a whole, and when the participation of specialized company functions has been outlined, it should not be necessary to belabor all the endless details of supporting planning by every activity of the business. There is an abundance of published information and experience concerning planning in these areas of specialization.

The next two chapters will therefore summarize the sequential elements of business planning and outline, in broad terms, the relations of the different functions of the business to each element. Subsequent chapters will then consider in more detail the activities involved in each element of this suggested business planning process.

The first activity, in time and importance, for which general management must make itself responsible in undertaking a program of long-range planning is an examination of the planning process. Through a study of its sequential elements a procedure can be outlined which will enable the business to anticipate and take advantage of its most profitable growth possibilities. This approach is basic to the most promising—if not the *only* effective—means of controlling costs, pricing, and in general operating a business successfully.

2. The Sequential Elements Of Business Planning

THE REQUISITES OF BUSINESS PLANNING ARE SUGgested in broad terms by our three fundamentals: the relation of the business as a whole to its parts, the crux of business success, and the concept we have called customer orientation. But what specific information is required, how should it be related and evaluated, what judgments and decisions are required, what actions and results should be programed, and how can all this be most meaningfully expressed and utilized in operating the business as a whole? Some answers to these questions can be derived from a summary identification of the sequential elements of business planning followed, in later chapters, by a more detailed look at each of them in turn.

AIMS AND ACTIVITIES

In order to establish any sound procedure or process it is necessary first to define specifically what is to be accomplished. By the same token, complete understanding of a procedure is dependent upon knowledge of its aims. It is shocking how many procedures exist in business which cannot be explained in terms of their aims even after they have been established and slavishly adhered to for years.

The more the business knows about the needs it is attempting to serve, the better chance it has to match or beat its competitors. No understanding, or only a superficial understanding, of these needs is an engraved invitation to disaster. A complete understanding can give us a running start on competition and can be gained through an organized attempt at identification in terms of specific performance, appearance, and economic factors *important to the customer.* The product and service requirements developed in this way provide a basic guide in at least two important respects if—as they should—they represent the practical ideal from the customer's standpoint. First, they constitute the only valid common denominator for comparing the business's current product with competitive products—the heart of today's sales story. Second, they determine the criteria for evaluating possible future product improvements or product substitutions by the company or its competitors.

The problems of any business in coming up with the product that will most satisfactorily fill a particular need, and which will therefore be the one favored by the customer, are complicated by the ever-changing nature of the customer's requirements due to economic, social, and political influences. Hence the fundamental challenge of anticipating and meeting these requirements—and doing so more readily and proficiently than anyone else.

Customers—Direct and Indirect

Although he has long been recognized as king, the customer's many-sided character or multiple personality may not in fact have been fully understood by those seeking to serve him.

Sound planning requires the broadest possible interpretation of the word "customer" so as to include not only direct and indirect customers but present and potential customers in both categories. *Direct* customers are those to whom the business offers its product (or service) for first use: say, Manufacturer *X* who purchases a part for incorporation in his own product or a housewife who buys an item for home use exactly as it is offered by the business. *Indirect* customers are all others in the channel of distribution down to and sometimes including the ultimate user of the product: wholesalers and retailers of the item bought by the housewife, for example, or the consumer-user of Manufacturer X's product.

Those to whom a business first sells or transfers its product, whether they are direct or indirect customers, have certain product and service requirements. In the rare case when they are direct customers and there are no indirect customers, the business will have the right product if it can meet those requirements. In all other instances, the product may not be right, since the indirect customers will have their own product and service requirements. The business must, in effect, strive to meet a composite of all their requirements in serving the customer need which they have in common.

A business which is blind to the requirements of the ultimate user or of any others in the channel of distribution is a sitting duck so far as its more perceptive, alert competitors are concerned.

Competitive Forces

The third key to the information-gathering activity, "competition," also should be broadly interpreted for sound planning.

Direct competition is that which comes from suppliers of other products which serve the same needs as one's own. These competitive items may be made of the same or different materials. *Indirect* competition is any other force which may decrease the sale of the business's products. It may take the form of new manufacturing techniques which reduce or even eliminate the demand for the kind of product offered by the business. The trend toward "do it yourself," for instance, indirectly makes competition for those dealing in certain products or services. According to a recent Census Bureau estimate, 23 per cent of the $13 billion spent annually for home repair and improvement is attributable to do-it-yourself homeowners.

DYNAMIC FUTURE SITUATION

The situation with which a business must grapple proficiently if it is to survive is highly dynamic, never static. Not only are the three elements—customer needs, customers, and competition—individually in a state of constant change, but they react on one another.

An understanding of the past situation, then, is obviously not enough, nor is an understanding of the present. It is the future situation which is important to the future of the business. Knowledge of the past and the present is desirable only to the extent that it provides a perspective for judgments and projections.

Available Resources

When a business has attained a real understanding of its situation, a firm foundation has been laid upon which it can become truly customer-oriented. In a sense, it has looked outside and assessed the specific environment in which it hopes to operate successfully in the future. It must next assess itself, not in general or vaguely, but in terms of its current and potential capabilities as these relate directly and specifically to its situation. Capabilities depend upon the resources available to the business, and a knowledge of those resources in terms of their application to specific customer needs—that is, in terms of their market significance—is necessary for sound planning.

In other words, once management knows the environment in which it will operate, it must next understand what it will have to operate with.

Scope of the Business

A business must always be careful to stay within its proper sphere. Since it cannot hope to cover the universe, it should confine itself to that area represented by the particular customer needs which its capabilities are best suited to fill.

This area, for ready reference, can be called the "scope" of the business. The going will be tough enough within it, even when resources are fully applied. *Unconscious* or *unintentional* excursions beyond the business's proper scope are bound to be costly because at least one resource is always involved. That is *time,* the only resource that cannot be replaced.

A Defined Purpose

Every organization has a purpose, however poorly it may be defined or understood even by its members. Like the North Star, it can provide a timeless, constant fix to navigation for those who can relate their courses to it.

If it is to provide such guidance, purpose is best expressed in terms of the timeless intentions of the business as to the kinds of overall results desired: profit, growth, leadership, corporate citizenship. So defined, it serves as a fulcrum for the balance between customer needs and resources (see Chapter 1, Chart I).

A business without a clear understanding of its purpose is like a ship at sea in Columbus's time with clouds obscuring the North Star night after night. Even if it is lucky enough not to strike the reefs immediately, it still doesn't know where it is going.

A business with a defined purpose—a clear look at the North Star—checks this reference point before and during each tack. Its situation is the weather; its resources are the ship; its scope is the sea upon which it is sailing.

SELF-ANALYSIS

The necessary information is now complete. Except for updating its data and projections, the business requires no more basic raw material with which to formulate its plans. From this point on it is a matter of putting the separate pieces of information together in a manner which will be most meaningful for making decisions.

Sequential Distillation

The relationship of these pieces of information is indicated—and their use implied—by their very nature.

The picture we have obtained of the company's future *situation* shows the specific *customer needs* which will be in existence, who will have them, what their requirements will be, and how and by whom they will be served. Overlaying this picture with the profile of *resources* reveals what will be feasible for the business in this situation. Superimposing *scope* upon the result further limits discussion to products and services within the chosen area. And screening what is left against *purpose* discloses what is most worthy of serious consideration by the business.

This sequential distillation should bring out all the chances which the business will have to serve specific customer needs and permit management to isolate those with the most profitable growth potential for the business.

Identification of Opportunities

Through this process of outside-inside evaluation, a business should be able to line up the opportunities that are open to it. Once this has been done, all that remains from a planning standpoint is to decide which opportunities are to be pursued, how, when, and with what predictable results.

Each opportunity—that is, each chance to serve a specific customer need—must be identified in precise terms before any intelligent decision can be made. However, if management really understands its situation, resources, scope, and purpose, it knows:

- All the identified customer needs it can serve, plus the nature of each need in terms of product and service requirements both practical and ideal.
- The capabilities of the business in terms of those requirements.
- The magnitude and timing of each need.
- The magnitude and timing of each major means of serving each need.
- The direct and indirect customers who will have each need.
- The competitors of the business and their current capabilities as related to product and service requirements.
- The economic, social, political, and industrial influences which should be considered in serving each need.
- The kinds of results which the business as a whole must achieve in serving these needs.

Thus the business has in substance determined the location, dimensions, and principal characteristics of its "land of opportunity." Within this area, on the basis of the informed judgments it has already made, management is able to define individual opportunities in precise terms. "Precision," to be sure, is not synonymous with "accuracy." Every effort should of course be made to obtain the most accurate information available and to make the most accurate judgments and projections possible, but the point of diminishing returns is soon reached.

If a business is unable to serve a particular need and cannot acquire the required capability, that need holds no opportunity for it. If the business can, however, serve the need, it has an opportunity. If the business has several basically different capabilities—or ways of serving a need—it has several opportunities, and they should be evaluated and planned for separately.

Selection and Ranking: Strategy

Even when a business has identified all its opportunities, it will seldom be able to tackle them all. Certainly it cannot handle them all at once or with the same emphasis. Some device or guide is required for selection and ranking as to importance.

The precise identification of each opportunity will have revealed its nature and magnitude, both of which are vital considerations in selection and ranking. However, there is a more basic, although possibly more general, consideration which deserves special attention. That is the *strategy* of the business. Opportunity *A* may be of lesser magnitude than Opportunity *B* but still be more important to the business for strategic reasons. Strategy often rates one opportunity over others, as of a certain point in time, even though in some respects it is no different from the rest.

Every business has a strategy, conscious or unconscious, express or implied, formal or informal. If it is not clearly understood, it will be a source of misdirection rather than proper guidance in the selection of individual opportunities and the relative emphasis to be given them.

THE EVALUATION PROCESS

At this juncture the business is ready to evaluate more fully those opportunities which have survived thus far. It must decide exactly what it will do about each and what results it can expect.

Some opportunities may be too insignificant to deserve full evaluation. These should be so labeled and set aside. The chance of serving a particular need which is too small in dollars or units, as related to the facilities of the business, will fall in this category. All other opportunities should be evaluated individually, and as they concern one another, from the particular perspective of each and every function of the business before final decisions are made.

What are these functions, whether in a one-man or a multi-unit operation? At the risk of oversimplification, we may say in general that most businesses include a research and development function, in some sense, regardless of how important it may be in fact or how fully it may be recognized by management. This is also true of engineering. Obviously, too, if a business makes a product, rather than merely purchasing it for resale, a manufacturing function is required; and no business can exist without the financial and general management functions. A sales function has long been recognized; recently, as we have seen, it has been either supplemented by or included in a so-called marketing function. Finally, there is also a personnel function, however designated or organized, for any operation with more than one person, but for simplicity it will be ignored in this analysis.

How is the evaluation of opportunities to take advantage of the knowledge and experience represented by these company functions?

There will be no point to an evaluation of a specific opportunity by general management if in the view of all or any one of the other functions it will not be feasible to pursue that opportunity. There is no reason why the opportunity should be evaluated by finance if it is not feasible from a manufacturing, engineering, research and development, or marketing standpoint. Evaluation by manufacturing will be wasted if the opportunity is not feasible from an engineering, research and development, or marketing standpoint. Evaluation by engineering is an empty gesture unless the opportunity is feasible from the research and development and marketing standpoints. And it may be interesting but it will be useless to evaluate the opportunity from the research and development standpoint if it will not be feasible from the marketing standpoint.

This line of reasoning suggests that the sequence for functional evaluation is as follows: marketing, research and development, engineering, manufacturing, finance, and general management. This sequential evaluation, as will develop, is also cumulative.

The Marketing Evaluation

Recognizing marketing as the first evaluation, in point of time if not in importance, is consistent with our basic principle to the effect that planning begins in the marketplace.

Needless to say, this first evaluation should be made by those most familiar with the marketplace, presumably those responsible for the marketing function. For our purposes here, we shall assume that someone in the business—even if only the one man in the one-man organization—acts as a marketing planner. How does he evaluate each opportunity, and what is done with his evaluation?

Briefly, the marketing planner wants to determine the magnitude and timing of the opportunity, a possible way or ways in which it can be pursued by the business, and the results which can be predicted. A real understanding of situation will provide him with data as to the magnitude and timing of similar opportunities in the past and a sound basis upon which he can form a judgment as to the future. Situation also will point out clearly or at least provide clues to the kind of action which is appropriate. This action will concern one or more of our three information keys, because it will be aimed at the need, with its product and service requirements; at the customers; or at competition. This action, further, can be of two kinds: the sort taken by the business in the past, in the same or a modified form, or new action. In either event it will be dependent upon the resources of the business.

The marketing planner must consider, in addition, when the action should be taken and with what emphasis or priority as related to other action. The timing of the opportunity, and the actions of customers and competition anticipated in his study of the situation, suggest the judgments he must make—judgments which will also be influenced by the business's known present and anticipated future capabilities. His understanding of the available resources will generally give him the necessary knowledge of current capabilities and, to some extent, a knowledge of future capabilities as well. If, therefore, he has made a reasonable effort to understand the company's resources fully, the marketing planner should be able to play his part effectively in the business planning process. In any case, as will be seen, the later steps are so designed that any misdirections stemming from deficiency in his knowledge will be corrected automatically.

The marketing planner's analysis of what he believes can and should be done by the business, with what probable results, should be summarized in writing for use in evaluations by other functions. Where appropriate, alternatives should be indicated. Results should be stated as approximations or in ranges. Proposed action by the marketing function should be detailed; action suggested for others should be generalized except as certain critical results are concerned.

Thus this first evaluation reflects the view of the man or group with the most knowledge of the marketplace, the one with the most knowledge of the business's selling capabilities and a good, though possibly incomplete, understanding of its other capabilities.

Other Functional Evaluations

The fact that the marketing planner cannot be expected to have a complete understanding of all current and particularly all prospective capabilities, in all functional areas, calls for subsequent, interrelated evaluations. For example, these subsequent evaluations should show whether more or less product development can be expected than originally contemplated, whether greater or smaller quantities and costs can be anticipated, whether profits and the resulting funds available for operations will exceed or fall short of estimates. Without such knowledge, a sound decision to pursue or abandon an opportunity cannot be made.

The first evaluation of the marketing planner is therefore followed by one from the standpoint of research and development—but within the frame of reference provided by the marketing planner. Evaluation from the standpoint of engineering then follows, again within the frame of reference provided by the marketing planner but modified by R&D considerations. Next come evaluations by manufacturing and by finance, each within the framework established by previous analysis. The final evaluation—as well as the decision whether to pursue the opportunity, when, and how—is made by general management on the basis of the integrated judgment of all these different functions of the business.

General management's decision puts the final stamp on the results to be sought and the steps to be taken. If these have been developed in the manner outlined, general management will merely approve or modify the tentative results (objectives), and the supporting action programs (targets) suggested by the sequential and cumulative considerations we have seen are inherent in business planning.

OVERVIEW

The sequential elements of business planning—as summarily defined and explained to this point—are situation, resources, scope, purpose, opportunities, strategy, objectives, and targets.

Planning as a Pyramid

These elements can be meaningfully shown as a pyramid (Chart II). The base is situation—a composite of customer needs, customers, competition, and the major influences on their dynamic future. All the other elements depend and are built upon this base; changes in it should prompt re-examination of all the rest. Each succeeding element in turn depends and is built upon the one beneath it; similarly, a change anywhere should flag attention to the elements which follow (as will be obvious, too, where planning is depicted—more accurately—as a circle).

The pyramid shape also indicates that planning in this sequence is a narrowing process. Areas of consideration grow progressively smaller and move from the general to the specific. And the peak of attainment, the chart suggests, is profitable growth. Anything else, including planning, is merely a tool for achieving it.

The Focus of Planning

Chart III illustrates the importance of, and the reason for, the particular sequence we have suggested for the elements of business planning. It shows the progressive distillation of information, judgments, and decisions. The process "starts" in the marketplace and "ends" with specific scheduled action programs. Throughout, attention is directed to what is most important to the business. This

CHART II

THE PLANNING PYRAMID

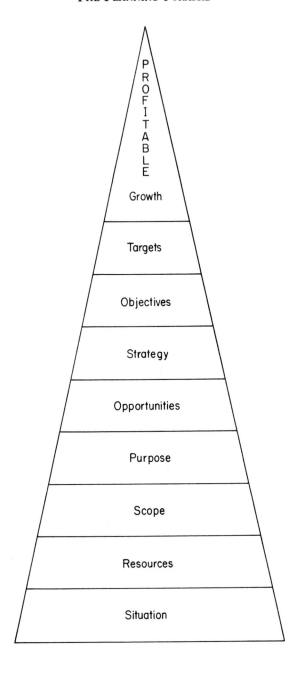

CHART III
TOTALITY OF CUSTOMER NEEDS

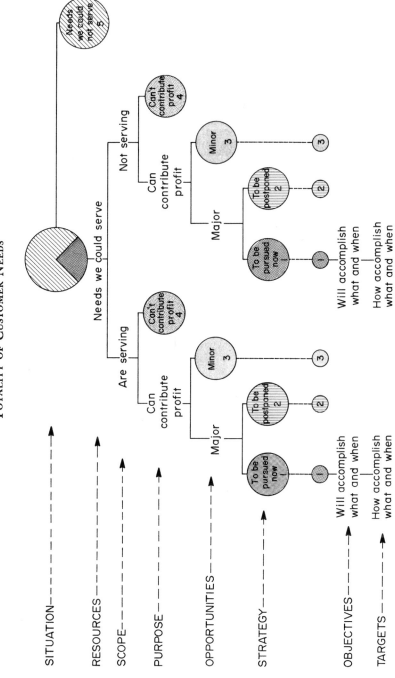

process should therefore help all company functions and general management as well to concentrate on matters according to their relative priority and to ignore the unimportant. To the extent this is accomplished, the process also constitutes a basic cost control system. As charted, all the available time and effort should first be given to the 1's and 2's; none should be wasted on the 5's and 4's.

The chart indicates why this process should be useful to those who recognize and want to achieve the aim of business planning: to anticipate, and program in all functions of the business, the future service of those customer needs with the most profitable growth possibilities for the business. It is not an end unto itself but only a means to assist or perhaps even force a business to answer the key question: "Where are we going?" Theodore Levitt states the facts succinctly:

> The answer to the question of where your company is and should be going depends on a lot of things. It depends on where the company has been, what its competence and strengths are, what the competition is doing, and what is happening out there in society and in the consumer's enigmatic mind.

> One thing we know for sure about society and consumers is that they are constantly changing in ways that are extremely important to every business. The trick is to anticipate and act on these changes before the competition does, and to do it at the right time and in the right way.[2]

Neither this suggested business planning process nor any other can substitute for judgment and vision. It can only supplement them. "The key to measuring a company's future lies not in its past record so much as in the quality and wisdom of the decisions that its management is making today."[3]

Neither this nor any other planning process, moreover, will guarantee that the results planned will be achieved. This process can and should make such results more obtainable—*or greater or lesser results consistent with the developing situation.*

Nor can this or any other process eliminate business risks. It

[2] *Innovation in Marketing*, McGraw-Hill Book Company, Inc., 1962, p. 12.
[3] *Forbes*, January 1, 1963, p. 58.

should aid in identifying and evaluating risks and thereby stimulate the assumption of more risks; that is, well-calculated and rewarding risks. As Bruce Payne explains:

> . . . A company [can] go further than it would otherwise dare to in taking advantage of its strengths. Management can safely extend itself more, get more mileage out of its assets, flex its muscles more. There is less holding back because of needless fears about how far and how fast the firm can go. We live in an expanding economy. Some companies need to expand at unprecedented rates just to stay in competition. Long-term planning, properly conceived, answers the question, "How fast should we grow?" It points up the obstacles to growth and prepares management to overcome them.[4]

[4] "Steps in Long-Range Planning," *Harvard Business Review*, March-April 1957, pp. 95-106.

Planning can and often does go on independently in every area of the business. Someone, clearly, must reconcile the varied efforts—a task that may be very nearly impossible. A device is needed to prevent them from taking off in all directions. The axis about which they must revolve? Opportunities for profitable growth.

3. The Functional Elements Of Business Planning

THE SEQUENTIAL ELEMENTS OF BUSINESS PLANNING dictate, to some extent, not only the timing but the nature of the contribution to be made by each functional area of specialization. What, when, and how each function performs its unique role in this process will be developed in the chapters to follow. However, it may be advisable to have an overall view of these functions' interrelationships before examining them in detail.

Such a view is provided by visualizing the suggested process in the form of a circle rather than as a straight line. The circle is most appropriate since real planning is continuous and includes feedback. Let us therefore take not one but three looks at this circle. The next three charts cannot fully come to life for the reader until he has read the chapters explaining each functional element of planning, but a quick review of their highlights should provide a background for later discussions.

The Common Axis

Chart IV shows the functional parts of the circle and the axis around which these parts should revolve. Planning by each function is, in a sense, separate and therefore is depicted as a separate circle. In theory, each function could do its planning separately, and their

CHART IV

THE AXIS OF SEPARATE FUNCTIONAL PLANNING

Planning by each function is separate and continuous and is therefore depicted as a separate circle. *Opportunities for profitable growth of the business as a whole* is the common focal point—or axis—around which planning in all functions should revolve.

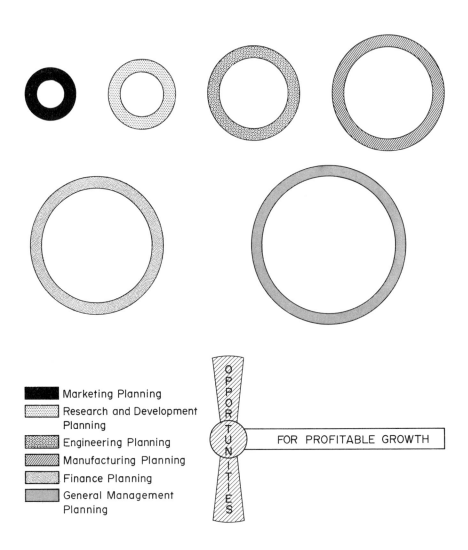

CHART V

SEQUENTIAL FLOW CHART OF BUSINESS PLANNING

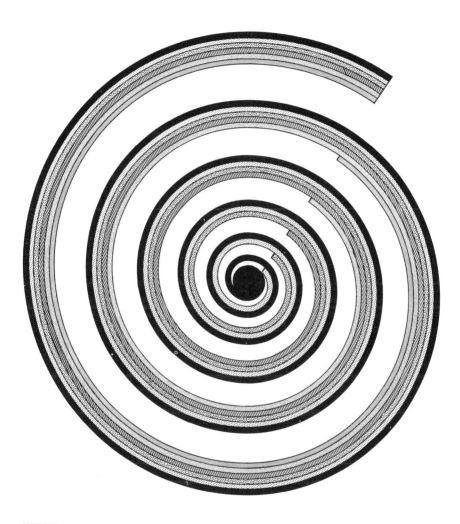

Marketing Planning
Research and Development Planning
Engineering Planning
Manufacturing Planning
Finance Planning
General Management Planning

output could then be brought together in some meaningful form. As a practical matter, this is next to impossible, although the practice is widespread in business today.

The device which prevents the separate parts of the circle from rolling off in all directions is the common axis around which they must revolve. This axis is *opportunities for profitable growth*; here is the obvious focal point for all planning. The implications for management have had vocal recognition, but the lack of impact on actual company practice is appalling—as a cursory examination of most development and engineering activities will prove. To prevent any misunderstanding, let it be added that in many, if not most, cases the fault does not necessarily lie with development and engineering personnel. It rests with others who fail to provide them with the required axis for their planning; who either don't know how to find it or can't put it to practical use.

Furthermore, if not only the planning but the activities of all the areas of specialization are to be coordinated by general management —as they must be—it is none too soon to start their integration at the planning stage. Efforts to integrate begun at a later date are likely to be less effective and certainly more expensive.

Sequential Flow of Planning

Chart V attempts to visualize what should happen when the functional parts of the circle are placed on, and revolved around, the lugged axis.

Thus business planning starts at the center with marketing planning. As opportunities are identified and evaluated by marketing in accordance with its understanding of situation, resources, scope, purpose, and strategy, proposals concerning their selection and pursuit— stated in terms of *tentative* objectives and targets—are offered for consideration from other functional standpoints: first research and development, then engineering, and so on.

The prime importance of marketing's role is suggested by Thomas A. Staudt of Michigan State University:

While all individual actions taken in the functional areas can be considered as within management discretion, *it is the market which*

CHART VI
BUSINESS PLANNING:
Interrelationships of the Major Components

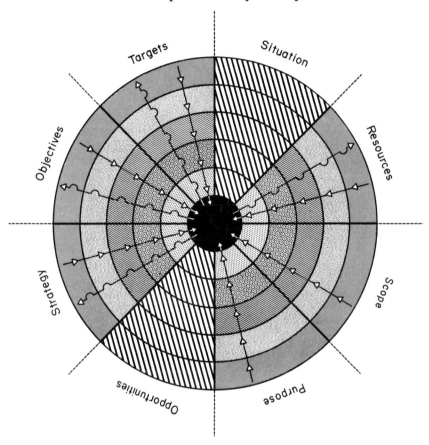

Marketing Planning

Research and Development Planning

Engineering Planning

Manufacturing Planning

Finance Planning

General Management Planning

sanctions all the preceding steps prior to the making of a sale. This is to say that *the market holds at least veto power over the entire system.* What is done in research and development, production design, production scheduling, quality control, inventory control, and the like must ultimately meet the test of the marketplace—do buyers give their approval through allocating their own resources for the purchase of the product in sufficient quantities and at adequate prices? Since this veto power exists and since the firm is organized for the purpose of profitably serving market opportunity, it follows that the *strategy and tactics of the firm should be market-oriented.**

When a proposal reaches general management for decision, as Chart V shows, it should have had the cumulative consideration of all functions, within a common frame of reference initiated by a careful look at the marketplace. If this is the case, general management's decision can be made only after taking all functional considerations into account. In addition, it will automatically finalize objectives and targets in all areas of the business *which are coordinated with one another.* The marching orders for the business are given in a manner that will get all functions into step. Integration is under way!

A Truly Integrated Effort

Chart VI is intended as a still picture of revolving Chart V. It should confirm the points previously noted and, in addition, suggest a few more.

Marketing planning is at the center; springing from it we see identification and first evaluation of the possible opportunities for profitable growth. Marketing's view of situation—whether it be complete or incomplete—is the basic understanding that the business has of customer needs, customers, and competition. All the other functions, including general management, must rely on it in their planning. Even though they can and should contribute refinements to this basic understanding, any lack of vision on the part of marketing is bound to permeate the whole process of business planning.

Each function contributes to the understanding of *resources,*

* "Business Management as a Total System of Action and the Role of Marketing," in *Managerial Marketing—Perspectives and Viewpoints* (revised edition), Eugene Kelley and William Lazar, editors, Richard D. Irwin, Inc., Homewood, Illinois, 1958, pp. 6-7.

but—to repeat—within the frame of reference originated by marketing from its reading of the *situation*. For example, an estimate of total yearly production capacity is meaningless if the opportunity in question involves only a seasonal demand. Or a forecast of engineering manpower and capability generally is meaningless if the opportunity involves product improvements of a particular kind within a specific period of time.

Top management decisions on *scope* are equally binding on all functions of the business in their respective planning activities. If scope defines, as it should, the area in which the business is to operate, all activities should concentrate on that area and not waste time, effort, and money wandering around in what may appear to be greener fields. If nothing else, such excursions will put them out of step with the other functions.

Purpose, as established by top management judgment and decision, is our guiding star. The timeless intentions of the business as a whole cannot be determined by each function separately. Basically, they should direct each function in all its planning and action.

It is the responsibility of marketing to identify all possible *opportunities*. Blindness or astigmatism on its part affects the entire business body. Marketing also suggests what the *strategy* of the business should be, though its view may be modified by those of other functions. Once a strategy has been approved by top management, it controls all functional planning and should lead in turn to functional strategies.

Marketing proposes the selection of certain opportunities and tentative *objectives and targets* for each. Within this framework, the other functions offer their individual considerations, their tentative objectives and targets. Final decisions are then made by general management, and these provide the basis for all action programs and their implementation.

*   *   *

To sum up: Planning for the business as a whole calls for a highly coordinated effort by all areas of specialization. For that reason alone it cannot be haphazard or incomplete on the part of any one function.

Planning for the business as a whole should receive some broad general management guidance from its inception and throughout its course. Plans are made final only through general management participation and decision.

Planning for the business as a whole should establish a sound foundation for integrating and measuring the future actions of all functions and controlling costs from the standpoint of each management specialty and that of the business as well.

PART TWO:

The Elements in Detail

The first step in the planning process calls for taking a look at the environment in which the business will be operating in the future. Judgments must be made concerning customer needs, customers, and competition. The problem for management is how the necessary information is to be developed, organized, and used.

4. The Three Facets of Situation

BUSINESSES, LIKE INDIVIDUALS, ARE LIKELY TO GET SO preoccupied with themselves that they lose touch with what is going on around them. An individual can exist, in a fashion, unto himself. A business cannot.

The most starry-eyed idealist or impractical mystic must conclude, after any thought at all on the subject, that a business can survive only to the extent it serves some needs. This we have seen. Service of one or more needs is the lifeblood of any business enterprise, and the fountainhead of this vitalizing substance is the environment. The enterprise itself contains the heart which pumps and circulates the blood.

It is well known that environment affects the development of individuals, but many people seem at times to overlook the much greater influence it has on the development of businesses. The more a business understands its environment, the better chance it has for profitable growth—up to a point. Too broad and deep a knowledge can be as confusing as too little can be misleading.

There are three keys which open the door to the required understanding and keep us from wandering in a labyrinth of details. They are the now-familiar customer needs, customers, and competition. If a business understands these three factors as they exist at present, and as they can reasonably be expected to develop in the future, it knows enough about the environment to begin its planning. This is the three-facet situation facing management.

Point of Entry: Basic Demand

Even though our look at environment is thus narrowed, the area of knowledge described is still broad for even a small business. It is certainly too complex to digest in one gulp; it should be obtained, organized, and utilized in pieces. However, if a piecemeal system is followed, the pieces must be such that they will fit together, finally, into a whole picture. Furthermore, it is desirable to start with the more significant pieces.

This progressive approach is very simple. The planner starts with what he then believes to be the most important product which the business is currently offering for sale or is developing for future sale. He asks the question: "What function does this product perform for those who buy it for their own use?"

The first answer is likely to be in general terms. For example, an electric stove cooks food; an engine drives a pump; a TV set provides visual entertainment; a boat is used for fishing or sailing. A component performs a certain function within a manufactured product; a material may give it strength or color.

The planner next asks: "What is the basic demand with which this function is associated or from which it is derived?" With the stove it is probably the demand for prepared food; with the engine, the demand for a power supply; with the TV set, the demand for entertainment.

In the case of the component part or the material, the basic demand can be identified only by looking at the final product into which it is incorporated. For example, formed steel to be used in manufacturing an electric stove is associated with the same basic demand as the demand for the stove itself.

Segmentation of the Demand

After the basic demand has been identified, it should be examined to determine its general nature and dimensions. For instance, the basic demand for the electric stove might be analyzed and visualized as follows.

Basic demand = Prepared food for humans

Prepared in the home	Prepared in commercial establishments		
	Hotels	Restaurants	Other

This basic demand can and should be divided into meaningful segments in order to understand it better. It may appear, with a little thought, that the basic demand for food prepared in the home may be somewhat different from that for food prepared in commercial establishments. These two segments are therefore identified. The home segment is considered first merely because the product presently sold or conceived seems more obviously connected with it. In addition, further segmentation of the total basic demand may be apparent, if not in the beginning, later in the course of planning. At least a door has been opened into which the planner may enter for more careful exploration.

The original segmentation may prove to have been in error. However, it will serve its purpose if it leads to the precise identification of customer needs, customers, and competition which is essential to a proper understanding of environment.

CUSTOMER NEEDS

People require many means for preparing food in their homes, ranging from equipment for cleaning, cutting, and mixing through storage for raw or semiprepared ingredients to facilities for heating and cooling. Our particular planner is interested only in those needs which can be met by the product he has available. This is the need for means of heating or cooking. He wants to know everything possible about this need, but he cares nothing about the others except to the extent that they may affect cooking.

Quantification in General Terms

Before spending a lot of time and effort studying the cooking need, the planner should get a general idea of its size. If it is small now and cannot be expected to grow in the future, he may decide to set it aside and look at another need, possibly one connected with preparing food in commercial establishments. He may follow the same procedure if the need is large now but for some reason will almost disappear over the next decade. If, on the other hand, the need is growing, his interest is sharpened.

The planner therefore tries to quantify his needs *not precisely but generally*. Only a major miscalculation of size, or of direction and rate of growth, will be critical to the further consideration to be given it. In calculating its present and future magnitude, the planner may consult several sources of information and be forced to make many different kinds of judgments concerning future developments. If he is interested only in the United States, his job will be relatively easy; he will have ready access to government and industry statistics. If, however, his company is thinking of going overseas and he wants to know the extent of his need in specific foreign countries, his problem will be much greater.

Our planner may, for example, obtain statistics on the basis of which he can estimate the number of homes in existence now, those under construction now, and those in prospect for the future. He must then judge whether, and to what extent, the need for cooking in the home will diminish or increase for any reason other than the changing number of home units. He must take into account any trend toward apartment house dwelling, with only central cooking facilities, or—farfetched though it may appear at the moment—eating all meals "out."

In many cases, such a careful look at the segments of the basic demand will reveal that one segment is growing at the expense of others. At this point the planner may logically decide to concentrate on it.

Examination in Depth

Having determined the general size of the need, and on that basis having decided it is worth further, more careful, examination, the planner is now ready to study it in depth, to plan how it can be served by his business, and to recommend, possibly, that it should be. He will return to the basic demand perhaps many times in his search for additional needs to study—and to plan. But he can take only one at a time. He will "case" the situation for each need, and plan the service of each, separately.

A planner using this approach may find, either during or upon completion of his study and planning, that he has overfragmentized his work; that is, he has considered as two or three needs what is, in fact, only one. No harm has been done, however. At the cost of a little extra work, he has simply identified the true need and learned its requirements and possibilities more precisely than he might have otherwise. He merely consolidates his findings, and in future planning he considers only the single need.

On the other hand, the planner may find that his original concept of a need is too broad; that is, he is really considering several needs. But, since this discovery is bound to take place early in his study of the situation, all he has to do is to divide his planning into the pieces indicated.

All these possibilities that face a planner in his first application of this approach suggest that it is essentially a "cut and try" method. Indeed, the initial "entry" into the suggested process is intentionally so. This is the best way to gain a real understanding of customer needs. It also is very useful in dispelling the preconceived notions of people with long experience in the business which can be both an asset and a handicap in planning. The superficial knowledge that might be obtained by slide rule, say, would be more dangerous than helpful.

To study a need in depth and plan for it in detail, the planner must progressively sharpen his understanding. To this end, he should describe it in writing, in as definitive terms as possible. In the case of the electric stove, for example, he should at this stage be thinking of something far more specific than "cooking food." His look at the basic demand should have led him to think more or less as follows: "Housewives need means of cooking family portions of food, quickly, safely, conveniently, and economically." Such a definition should suffice for the moment and be recorded for further development.

CUSTOMERS

The planner is now ready to identify precisely who has this need—customers, present and potential. His recognition of housewives as belonging to this group is only the beginning of wisdom.

  b. Emphasis on innovation in their own products and on innovation by their suppliers.
  c. Attitude toward self-supply.
  d. Buying habits—timing and location of purchasing, manner of purchasing, basic purchasing policies and practices.

  > *For example:* It is a major problem for all stove manufacturers to introduce a new or fresh look and unique features into their products periodically. They devote a great deal of effort to this problem themselves, and they favor suppliers who share their concern. They are not likely to consider making rather than buying new components unless they are of an electrical nature. As a group, they prefer to have at least two sources of supply for all components. Most of them make long-term commitments through a central purchasing group, but individual factories order against this according to their requirements.

B. Major individual direct customers

  1. Who and where are they, now and in the future, and what are their shares in the market associated with this need?
  2. In very summary terms, what other markets do they serve— productwise and geographically?
  3. What individual characteristics do they have which are significant in terms of this need?
  4. What corporate or other form of close relationships do they have which may be significant to the service of the need?
  5. What are their growth and profit trends, in total and with respect to the specific parts of their businesses relating to this need?

  > *For example:* Company X is the historic leader in its industry, but in recent years its share of the stove business has been decreasing because of new interests and efforts in other business fields. If, for some reason, a component supplier can serve only a limited number of customers, he may well choose Companies Y and Z, which are aggressively moving up.

The answers to all these questions concerning both indirect and direct customers should of course reflect any influences stemming from economic, social, and political factors and from basic trends and developments in the industries in which they participate.

Precise Magnitude of Need

The planner is now ready to determine the magnitude of his need —not generally, as he did earlier, but in precise terms.

Precision does not necessarily imply accuracy although, of course, accuracy is most desirable. In many instances it is not difficult to determine past and present magnitude accurately. In all cases it is impossible to be accurate with respect to future magnitude. But there is no reason why the planner cannot be accurate enough for sound planning.

How accurate is this? It varies with circumstances. In the absence of a crystal ball, the business planner has only two alternate courses of action open to him. He can make some assumptions based on hunch or daydreams, or he can try to project future magnitude on the basis of the best thinking available, organized and directed to the question and the factors which affect the answer. The choice is so obvious that one wonders why it is so seldom followed.

If the planner has carefully studied his need, he should be in a position to make a reasonable projection of its future magnitude. His efforts should represent, at the very least, a projection in yearly units or dollars which attempts to take into account those known factors which are most likely to be significant. With this, plus a statement of the major influences on it and the judgments and reasoning behind it, the planner can obtain confirming or modifying opinions from others knowledgeable in the business. Such a supporting statement will facilitate observation of future developments and their immediate reflection in the projection of magnitude.

One may properly question the validity of a projection made in this way as the basis for planning business action. However, the problem is brought into truer perspective by asking, "What degree of error would prompt a major change in plans—and when?" More often than not, the planner will conclude, and rightly, that even if the projection should prove to be substantially in error, its wrongness would not signal any major change in plans, either new or for some time to come. During this time a further effort to read the future can be made.

Product and Service Requirements

A decision can here be made as to whether the need deserves further exploration by the business. For example, it may be of such a size as to interest only a job-shop operation, or it may be big now but with every prospect of decreasing noticeably over the next few years. If, from the standpoint of size, the need does interest the company, more details are in order regarding the kind of products and associated services which will satisfy it. Prior to this point, any consideration of these requirements, except in the most general terms, would have been unnecessary and wasteful. However, *from this step forward, a careful, detailed, thorough, and competent determination of product and service requirements is critical to sound planning and its implementation by all functions of the business.* The planner, in essence, is now at a major crossroads. If he takes the right road, he will find a smooth surface and his progress will be fast. If he chooses the wrong one, he will have to double back later or continue slowly over rough terrain.

Customer needs which do not demand a product but can be satisfied by services only have specific requirements concerning those services. Every customer need which can be served by a product has requirements concerning the product itself and, possibly, some which concern services associated with the purchase or use of the product. A business cannot know whether it is, or can become, qualified to serve a need without knowing what these requirements are. Incomplete knowledge on this score can mislead management into inappropriate and costly ventures or at least dull its success.

How can these requirements be determined for use in planning and operating a business? Both kinds—product-associated and service-associated—must be examined, preferably in a detailed analysis which considers each kind separately but which takes into account their relationship to one another. This understanding of product and service requirements will, however, be inadequate if it does not encompass the practical ideal from the customer's point of view. The customer is both judge and jury in deciding to what extent any offering by a business satisfies his need. He may have a very refined or only a vague idea of what his requirements are. In either event, a business trying to serve the need should have a refined and complete knowledge of them.

Such a knowledge is not gained simply by perusing a particular customer's product and service specifications—regardless of their completeness. Issued with a request for a bid or attached to an order or contract, they may show clearly what will satisfy that customer at the moment. This is most important to today's sales, which, presumably, were planned in the past. But the planner and his associates in the business are primarily interested in the future, and the customer's future specifications will evolve from his practical ideal. Thus anyone knowing the practical ideal can work toward anticipating future specifications. The more he knows, the more he will be in a position to develop improved products and services and, if necessary, make customers aware of their own requirements.

Not only is a complete understanding of the practical ideal necessary to future product development, but it can be a valuable sales tool. The customer's requirements are the only valid criteria against which to measure current product offerings in comparison with competitive offerings. Too often, as a simple story illustrates, management may be flying blind. The president of a small town's biggest manufacturing establishment habitually walked by a jewelry store on his way to work each morning. He always checked his watch by the clock in the window so that he could blow the factory whistle on time. One day he met the jeweler and told him proudly of this daily routine, whereupon the jeweler said, "That's very interesting. For years I've been setting my clock by your whistle."

The phrase "practical ideal" means what will be ideal *over the planning period,* from the customer's standpoint, within the realm of practicality, taking into account known developing technologies as well as social and economic trends. Nothing but frustration is gained by gazing at the impossible. The planner must remember, also, to examine the customer's multiple personality and to reflect the composite requirements of both direct and indirect customers. Their respective requirements must be analyzed in parallel. It may appear initially that the requirements of one group are in conflict with those of another. These, however, must be reconciled; they are not, or cannot continue to be, inconsistent.

Needs which are served by a product rather than a service generally have requirements which might be described and analyzed under the following or similar headings:

From standpoint of indirect customers		From standpoint of direct customers	
Consumer User	Retailer	Manufacturer	Composite

I. *Product requirements*

   A. Performance, covering such items as

        capacity   strength
        size   convenience
        weight   safety

    For example: Assume again the case of the component supplier for the stove manufacturer. If that component were a shelf for the oven unit, from the consumer's standpoint it would have to be of a size and shape to fit easily and snugly into the particular dimensions of the oven when being used by the housewife—and be easy to remove for cleaning. Requirements from the retailer's standpoint are certainly the same. The manufacturer should be concerned not only with original installation but with removability.

   B. Appearance, covering such items as

        design   size
        color   shape

    For example: The design and color of the shelf must not only harmonize with the manufacturer's design and color for the oven unit but also show as little grease stain as possible while in use by the housewife and be easily cleaned.

   C. Economy, covering such items as

        price   freight
        terms   cost of use

    For example: The shelf supplier's price must not exceed the stove manufacturer's cost limit, but it must permit enough built-in quality that the housewife will be able to count on a reasonable life expectancy for the shelf.

II. *Service requirements*

   A. Delivery, covering such items as

        time   location
        quantity   manner

    For example: The shelf manufacturer must be prepared to supply shelves in the quantities and at the times and places required by the stove manufacturer's production and replacement schedules.

   B. Assistance, covering such items as

        application engineering   finance   marketing

    For example: The stove manufacturer may design his product completely but expect application engineering assistance in the oven unit and its accessories.

These requirements should be identified and described in functional terms, or in terms of end results. This is an attempt, not to write engineering specifications for the ideal product, but to describe what functions—in detail—the ideal product would perform, how it would look, what its economics would be, and what services should be linked with its purchase and use. From this basic information, engineering and other specifications can later be drawn.

Basic Means of Service

With this complete or at least fuller knowledge of product and service requirements, the planner can better identify and understand the different ways in which his need has been served in the past and project how, basically, it will be served in the future. He is not yet ready to consider these basic means of service *in detail*; that would call for a definite product-by-product analysis. At this stage he should, however, know what essentially different means have been used successfully, the extent of their success, and the reasons for it— all of which information, combined with previously developed data, will give him a basis for judgment as to the future.

For example, our electric stove manufacturer's planner might find that over the past ten years his basic means of service have been wood/coal stoves, gas ranges, and electric ranges. He might find (to use purely hypothetical figures) that wood/coal stoves are now serving 5 per cent of the need, having dropped from 10 per cent; that gas ranges, after a decrease from 45 to 30 per cent, have recently leveled off at that figure; and that electric ranges, since a substantial increase from 45 to 65 per cent, also have steadied. If he knows the reasons for this historical development and adds to it his knowledge of customers, magnitude of the need, and product and service requirements, all evaluated in the light of political, economic, and social influences, he should be able with some assurance to estimate future overall trends in these and possibly new basic means of service. He might then conclude that wood/coal stoves will not drop below 3 per cent, that gas ranges will hold between 25 and 30 per cent, that electric ranges will continue between 65 and 70 per cent, but that an increasing proportion of these electric ranges will be electric/electronic.

If he has not already discovered that "the need for means of cooking family portions of food quickly, safely, conveniently, and economically" can and should be considered as several needs, rather than one, he should reach that conclusion now. He will certainly find that, among other things, outdoor grills have been sold in increasing quantities, as have special electric indoor roasters. These facts should lead him sooner or later to define the special cooking needs for which these products are offered as separate from the one he is currently studying. Their impact on it, if any, must be considered, but they deserve special study and planning of their own.

Here is an instance of the corrective stimulant inherent in the sequential considerations and other elements of the planning process. This type of correction is most likely to be triggered either in estimating the magnitude of the need or in determining its product and service requirements. Of course, if the stove manufacturer had defined the need he was serving more narrowly and accurately in the first place, these other cooking needs would have been noted but set aside for later examination.

COMPETITION

The stove man's planner was looking broadly at competition when he examined the basic means by which his need had been, and is now being, served. Similarly, in looking ahead, he must anticipate future competition. His conclusions regarding the future may be sound, but he cannot rely upon them until he has verified or modified them by the careful study and evaluation of competition which he must also bring to bear on the question to be faced later: "What should the business try to do about this need? How and when?"

This necessary understanding of competition, the third key to situation, is provided by the answers to the following questions:

I. *Direct competitors* (offering products made of the same basic materials as those made by the business)

    A. Major individual direct competitors

        1. Who and where are they?

Their locations, and particularly their proximity to customers, in comparison to the planner's location indicate not only their relative ability to make uninterrupted or quick deliveries but the cost of doing so, which may have important pricing implications.

2. What other markets, in general terms, does each serve—productwise and geographically?

    Their interests and efforts may be of an entirely different nature and timing if they are concentrating on one or a few needs than if they are spreading their energies—particularly where these additional needs are in several unrelated fields.

3. What are their individual characteristics with respect to the following?

    a. Capacity in total, and by important geographic areas, as related to this need; past, present, and future expectations.

    As indicated, a move by competition to locate production capacity closer to an area where the need is expanding certainly indicates new pressures calling for countermeasures.

    b. Growth in dollar volume and profit in total and, if possible, with respect to this need; past, present, and future expectations.

    Any continued loss in either volume or profits, or both, must eventually trigger some different action by that competitor.

    c. Emphasis on product innovation; past, present, and future expectations.

    Any awakening, or relapse, in product innovation activity by competitors will present either increasing problems or more favorable opportunities.

    d. Cost structure and trends; general understanding of past, present, and future expectations.

    Substantial improvement, or deterioration, in competitive cost structure signals a variety of possibilities ranging from drastic changes in prices to a surge in new product development or competition in new markets.

    e. Pricing; past and present publicly indicated philosophy regarding basic pricing problems—and future expectations.

    If competition favors cost-plus pricing, knowledge of competitive costs provides some basis for anticipating competitive pricing. Whether competition makes a practice of "following" or "leading" in price changes must also be considered.

    f. Quality standards; past, present, and future expectations.

Substantial improvement, or decrease, in competitors' quality standards introduces an infinite number of possibilities for action on the part of competition and the planner. Initially it may find expression primarily in pricing. In time it must lead to product improvement or product innovation.

4. What are the known major marketing and business problems of each competitor, insofar as they concern the service of this need?

If the chief problem is capacity and the competitor has capital readily available, that is one thing. If the problems relate primarily to management, that is another.

5. What are the known marketing policies and plans of each concerning this need?

If competition has announced or indicated in any way that it is aiming at one segment of the market, rather than the whole, plans can be laid accordingly.

B. Other direct competitors using the same basic materials, considered as a class

1. Who and where are these other direct competitors? Aside from their general description, where are they located, and what is their total share of the market for this need?
2. What are the prospects for additional direct competitors?
3. Consider these direct competitors as a group, along with those covered individually. What common characteristics do they have which are particularly significant to the service of this need? If nothing more, summarize their composite characteristics.

C. Direct competitors (offering products made of different materials)

1. Major individual competitors. (Same questions as for major direct competitors offering products of the same basic materials.)
2. Others in this group, considered as a class
   a. See B1.
   b. See B2.
   c. See B3.
   d. In the past, how successful has this group of direct competitors been in serving this need as compared with those which use the same basic materials as the planner? What expectations are there for the future? Why?

   For example: At one time glass container manufacturers competed principally with one another in serving the needs of brewers for means of containing individual consumer portions of beer and ale. Tin container manufacturers moved into the picture aggressively with a convenience (no-return) tin package and became the dominant factor in the market. The glass manufacturers, in recent years, have responded to this challenge with a one-way or no-return beer bottle. Similar prospects are now in view in the soft drink field.

Both types of manufacturers must understand and take into account the capabilities and probable actions not only of their counterparts in tin or glass but of their other very real competition. In the future, both may be sorry if they do not watch developments in other materials, such as plastics and composites using foils.

D. Indirect competition; forces, if any, other than those generated by direct competition which decrease the demand for products to serve the need in question

The classic examples of this indirect competition are the stories about the buggy whip and the long red flannel underwear. When the automobile replaced the horse-drawn carriage, the need served by the buggy whip all but disappeared. Similarly, with improved heating for homes and public places and some changes in social habits, the demand for heavy underwear has decreased substantially.

With technological developments accelerating in almost all fields of endeavor, with social and economic changes taking place at an increased pace, every business must keep a keen weather eye open for possibilities beyond the horizon of its direct competition.

Answers to all these questions about competition, like those concerning customers, should reflect influences stemming from economic, social, and political factors and from trends and conditions in the industries in which the competitors participate.

SUMMARY

THE CHANGING ENVIRONMENT

Upon completing his study of the situation, the planner should have a recorded analysis of the most important facts concerning present and past customers, which among their needs can be served by the business, and other companies that can serve those needs.

These facts include data as to size and number and details as to characteristics and requirements. They also include notes on major past influences. In addition, the planner has recorded projections of these same data for the full planning period. His judgments concerning the future are not facts in the true sense of the word, but until corrected by greater knowledge, by superior judgment, or by actual developments, they must be treated as factual for planning purposes. What better basis for guidance is available?

This first step in the planning process, in summary, is designed to "get a fix" on the environment within which the business will be operating over the planning period. It includes a procedure for organizing information on the current environment and judgment as to the future environment, both of which breed opportunities for the business and indicate the nature of the problems that will be encountered.

All aspects of the business environment may be of interest, and complete knowledge of them can be helpful. However, a basic understanding of certain aspects is essential to (1) early and complete perception of opportunities and (2) their pursuit in the most profitable manner for the business. These essential aspects are, of course, the three discussed at length in this chapter: the customer need or needs to be served by the business, the customers themselves, and the competition that can be expected. The more that is known about these three the better; "educated opinion" concerning them is a "must." If the essential data are developed, organized, and recorded in the sequence and manner suggested, the total should be not only more useful but less encumbered with interesting though not necessarily controlling information.

To repeat: Particular attention must be given to those underlying influences which have been important in the past and which will shape the future. Not that the company planner must have a complete knowledge of *all* the broad economic, social, and political factors, worldwide, national, and regional. Nor does he have to know the basic trends and conditions in *all* the industries in which his firm's customers and competitors participate. But he should understand those which have had or may have a major impact on the nature of the customer need to be served, who will have that need, and how and by whom it can be served. And *these influences should be analyzed as early as possible in the planning process in order that they may be reflected in each part of the situation to which they apply.*

In his article "Keys to Corporate Growth,"[1] Robert B. Young reports some highlights from the Stanford Research Institute's continuing study of the basic causes of corporate growth. After stating that "one of the most fundamental characteristics of the 100 high-growth companies studied is an affinity for growth fields," and that a critical task in long-range planning is "the early identification and interpretation of the basic reasons why growth fields emerge and change," Mr. Young continues:

> There are, of course, many reasons why a line of business may become a growth field. In the final analysis, however, these reasons will nearly always be embodied in the word *change*—sometimes a change involving technical innovation improving a firm's ability to supply a need; sometimes a change in the need itself. When the latter occurs, factors are at work entirely outside a company that will inevitably affect its future—factors that are often disguised and not recognizable as practical decision-making considerations.

> These factors are parts of what might be called the basic business environment which surrounds every company, market, and economy, and which ultimately governs changes in the demand for every product and service. The business environment represents a complex of shifts in the structure of society and the economy, in the state of technology, in the needs and tastes of people in the marketplace, in the policies and requirements of governments, and in the state and character of international tensions. In short, it is the sum of all the factors outside the control of a company's management which can change, and when changing carry with them sizable dollar impacts on the markets for particular goods and services.

Very few companies, Mr. Young observes, "show evidence of recognizing as a practical business guideline" the seemingly elementary conclusion that *"environmental changes are the starting point in the process of growth; they act as the stimulus that increases the opportunities for growth, without the help of which a company is fighting difficult odds."*

To cope with its changing environment, Mr. Young suggests that management should first establish a program for consistently "moni-

[1] *Harvard Business Review*, November-December, 1961, pp. 51-62.

CHART VII
ROAD MAP OF BUSINESS PLANNING

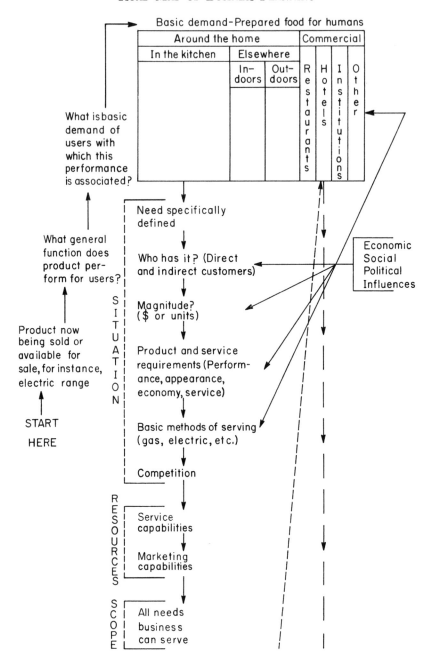

Basic demand-Prepared food for humans

Around the home			Commercial			
In the kitchen	Elsewhere		R e s t a u r a n t s	H o t e l s	I n s t i t u t i o n s	O t h e r
	In-doors	Out-doors				

What is basic demand of users with which this performance is associated?

What general function does product perform for users?

Product now being sold or available for sale, for instance, electric range

START HERE

SITUATION

Need specifically defined

Who has it? (Direct and indirect customers)

Magnitude? ($ or units)

Product and service requirements (Performance, appearance, economy, service)

Basic methods of serving (gas, electric, etc.)

Competition

RESOURCES

Service capabilities

Marketing capabilities

SCOPE

All needs business can serve

Economic
Social
Political
Influences

CHART VII
(Concluded)

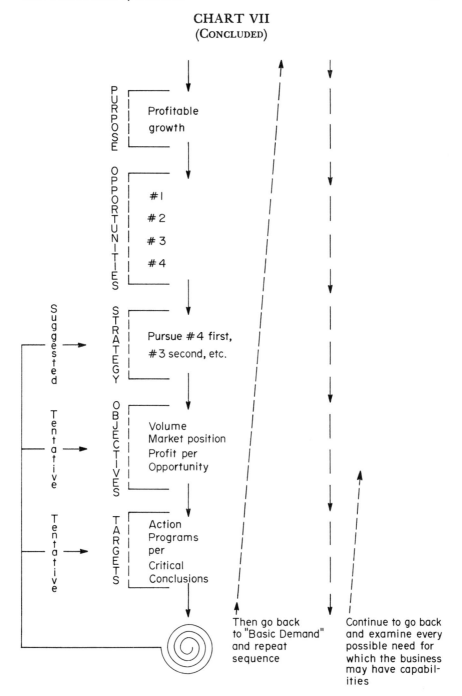

PURPOSE — Profitable growth

OPPORTUNITIES — #1, #2, #3, #4

STRATEGY — Pursue #4 first, #3 second, etc.

OBJECTIVES — Volume, Market position, Profit per Opportunity

TARGETS — Action Programs per Critical Conclusions

Suggested → Strategy

Tentative → Objectives

Tentative → Targets

Then go back to "Basic Demand" and repeat sequence

Continue to go back and examine every possible need for which the business may have capabilities toring" it like an early-warning radar system. Second, a means must be developed for "the sensing of innovative ways of fulfilling a growing need," or ways to seize the opportunities and avoid the threats.

The ground covered by the planner in his study of the situation, and the manner in which he approaches his work, are shown in Chart VII. The procedure is explained in terms of the electric stove without any attempt at accuracy concerning the basic demand or its proper segmentation. The chart is called a "road map" because it indicates the important guideposts along the route to better business planning.[2]

The planner starts with something "tangible," his product. If this is his first planning effort, that product should be the one he believes will be most important to the company's future. It may be on the market or in the last stages of development. The planner's first task is to become mentally attuned to it. Then, following the procedure outlined, he completes the first business planning step: the analysis of situation. Having done this, he knows that he is on the right track and he can proceed with subsequent steps.

The planner knows too that when he has finished the course for this particular activity or demand, he ought to explore other possible needs which may be satisfied by the same product or service but more likely will require a modified product or service.

---

[2] The road map shows, and anticipates, the other sequential elements of business planning which follow the situation step. It cannot, therefore, be understood fully until these other elements are examined further.

A superficial assessment of company capabilities is not very helpful and can be misleading. A careful assessment is based upon an inventory and evaluation of all resources in every area of the business. The focus is provided by the planner's detailed knowledge of needs, customers, and competition.

5. Examining the Available Resources

AGAINST THE CLEAR PICTURE HE HAS OBTAINED OF the situation which the business is facing, the planner must next evaluate the ability of the business to cope with it.

He must know to what extent the business is now capable of meeting specific product and service requirements. Subject to confirmation or correction by others in the business, he must also be able to anticipate its future capabilities. He must know how effective it is, and will be, in establishing contact with customers and maintaining the relationships with them that are required by their individual characteristics and problems. And he must know, at least in general terms, the relative capabilities—current and prospective—of its competition.

These capabilities of the business are a product of its resources. They are to be found in all company areas.

Functional Capabilities

Of both a tangible and an intangible nature, resources range from manpower to factories, from location to reputation. Each function is interested in developing and preserving those that are necessary, in its opinion, to perform its assigned duties.

Manufacturing is interested in production facilities and thinks in terms of square feet, numbers of machines, and man-hours of labor. Engineering is interested in technical knowledge and thinks in terms of numbers of specially trained personnel and engineering facilities. Marketing is concerned with customer contact and, therefore, with numbers, locations, and skills of field sales and service personnel. Marketing should also be alert to obtain and keep current all the information concerning customers and competition which is required to make the business truly customer-oriented; hence it should likewise be thinking of the manpower, skills, and information sources which this responsibility implies.

Management in each functional area of the business is responsible for planning and utilizing its own resources in an optimum manner *within that area*. The assessment of capabilities with which we are concerned here assumes a different standpoint and different terms. It is, of course, facilitated by a complete, current knowledge of resources in each specialization, and it should play a most important role in guiding their future development, as well as in planning for the business as a whole.

Resources in Combination

General management is responsible in its planning for utilizing *all* the company's resources—particularly in combination. Over and beyond these, however, the planner is interested *in certain capabilities resulting from the combination of all resources*—that is, capabilities which are directly and specifically related to needs, customers, and competition. He must know the strengths of the business from this standpoint in order to recommend what action should be taken by the business in the future.

It is the marketing planner who is expected to know most about the company's situation and so is presumably most interested in these joint capabilities. However, the manager of each functional specialization and general management as well must know the full potential of the business in terms of needs, customers, and competition in order to assure that the resources in their areas of responsibility which are required by the situation will be properly developed, maintained, and applied, *and that their energies will not be dissipated in the development and maintenance of other resources*. Business planning, in short, should be a device for matching existing and prospective resources with customer needs and, on that basis, directing their utilization or disposition. Happy is the management that is able to approximate this goal. Under our free enterprise system, the other type of management—which hardly perceives, much less achieves, such an objective—cannot long exist.

The full value of any business resource is realized only through its optimum application in the service of a customer need. And even a business which has matched all its resources with customer needs cannot utilize those resources to full advantage without also knowing and taking into account the relative capabilities of competition. No business can exploit unique capabilities effectively if it is not aware of them.

NEED-RELATED ANALYSIS

This all-important understanding of resources and the capabilities they represent can be best obtained and communicated to all concerned by an analysis *specifically related to each identified need.* This analysis should cover at least the following points:

I. *Product capabilities*

A. Technological. What research, development, and engineering personnel, facilities, and know-how are on hand or readily attainable or can be anticipated in the future? What technological areas of work, interest, and experience are represented, and what are the prospects for each? To what extent can the resulting capabilities satisfy any technical aspects of the product and service requirements? How does competition, in general, compare? What are the prospects here?

For example: Assume that Company *A* is competing with Company *B* and that their products must have certain performance characteristics, which depend upon knowledge and a high degree of skill in both metallurgy and electronics. Company *A* is at a distinct disadvantage if it has superior resources in metallurgy but practically no resources in electronics whereas *B* has balanced resources in both areas.

B. Production. What is the available capacity, current and prospective, by kind and location? What is the quality of production? To what extent can company capabilities satisfy the product and service requirements and maintain the necessary volume? How does competition, in general, compare?

For example: Assume that Company *A* and Company *B* are both prospective suppliers of a component needed by Company *C*. They have equal technological capabilities, but their production facilities are different in kind and in their location as related to *C*. If *C*'s expected production rate is 1,000 a week throughout the year and *A*'s capacity is the same, but *B* has a capacity of 1,200 a week, *B* has the necessary "safety factor" and therefore is in a better position, from the production standpoint, to serve *C*'s need. On the other hand, this advantage might be partly or fully offset if *A*'s factory were in the same city as *C*'s and *B*'s factory were a thousand miles away.

II. *Service capabilities.* What requirements do customers have as to quantity, time, or manner of delivery, currently and in the future? What kind and quality of assistance do they demand? To what extent can company capabilities satisfy product and service require· ments? How does competition, in general, compare?

For example: Company *A* (see above) would have an advantage if daily deliveries were required by *C*.

One sees today, throughout American business, a new awakening to the fact that the transaction is by no means "over" once a product is sold or a service is rendered. Management has long been aware of this, yet its response—at least in the consumer goods area—has been mostly negative, taking the form of warranties or guarantees whose real purpose is to limit responsibilities after the sale. Now its thinking is changing. The automobile companies, to cite one case, are beginning to realize that they are not just selling automobiles but are serving certain transportation needs.

Through force of circumstances (that is, the need to maintain a supply position), businesses which provide materials or components to other businesses have, in contrast, known for much longer that delivery often marks the beginning instead of the end of the transaction. A good supplier must be able to assist his customer in solving technical problems associated with a material or component. This assistance may involve the efforts of the supplier's research, engineering, and manufacturing departments, and it will, in the future, become more rather than less important. The truly customer-oriented business will not only develop and utilize its capabilities in this direction but will organize and act so as to anticipate and minimize the occasion for assistance *after delivery*.

III. *Marketing capabilities.* What kind of field sales and service personnel is needed? What other marketing personnel, facilities, and know-how? Where should they be located? Now and in the future? What are the firm's reputation and standing with customers, present and anticipated? How does competition, in general, compare?

For example: Some of the larger companies in the country, and even some smaller companies, spend a great deal of effort and money to blanket all markets with highly qualified field sales and service personnel. Yet, in doing so, they actually erect barriers to customers' orders in the form of overdecentralization of the organization, at least from the customers' standpoint. It is just possible that a customer may not want to go to the trouble of placing ten purchase orders with ten different offices at ten different locations when one order should suffice.

Technological, production, and service capabilities of the kind described can be superior to those of competition, but they will be of no value to anyone until, first, the business understands and applies them in terms of customer needs and, second, the customers understand and accept these applied capabilities in the service of their needs. Several kinds of skills are therefore indicated, presumably in the specialized area of marketing. For instance, provision must be made not only for the marketing planning outlined in this and the preceding chapter, but also for bringing the company's capabilities to the attention of customers through the face-to-face contact of skilled sales personnel and through effective advertising and sales promotion media. Capabilities in this latter area are important to most businesses and are considered critical in many, particularly those dealing in consumer products like soap and tobacco.

What about reputation? Of course, all businesses want a good one, but "good" can be defined in many ways and from many different viewpoints, whether those of the Federal Government, the local community, or competition. The reputation of importance to us here is the one (or ones) that the company has with current or prospective customers, and it also must have some bearing upon the specific need for whose standpoint the company's capabilities are being assessed. A reputation as a manufacturer, say, of high-quality kitchen appliances will not mean very much in communications but should be most valuable in the general field of household equipment. And of course some reputations are of value with respect to many or all needs—for example, having fine, aggressive salesmen who know their product is certainly a widely useful resource. But how much more valuable and generally applicable this kind of reputation would be if it also included a name for continuous sales order solicitation and order service, in terms of customers' present needs, and continuous inquiries and interest concerning future needs!

IV. *Time capabilities*, analyzed from at least two viewpoints
   A. Time of people. How much of the time of all interested people in the business can be devoted to this need?
   B. Timing of the business. How must the company time its actions in the possible service of this need? How does competition, in general, compare?

In a sense, people are probably the most important resource of any business. However, they can be replaced, even though at great expense and loss to the business. Another resource—*time*—cannot be replaced, and from that standpoint it is of first importance.

Time of People

A business's production facilities could have more capacity and be superior in practically every respect to those of competitors, and that business might still be completely or relatively lacking in production capability to meet a particular need. It might, for instance, be able to serve several needs from common facilities yet, for strategic reasons, choose to concentrate on certain needs and exclude others. Such circumstances, which must be taken into consideration in assessing production capabilities, point to a possible problem in manpower and organization, at any level and in any part of the business: Are enough people, and enough of their time, available for each need in view of all the needs to be served?

This problem is likely to be more obscure, as well as more important, the higher one goes up the organization ladder. For example, it should be obvious very quickly whether enough production workers of particular types are available, and it should not be difficult to determine whether there are enough specialists in engineering or sales. But what about general management and the managers of functional specializations? With each added level in the organization chart, it becomes increasingly necessary to take into consideration the probable allocation of these individuals' time and effort to some needs at the expense of others—a problem which is further accentuated by the perfectly human tendency of everyone to favor those matters of greatest personal interest.

Under the pressure both of circumstances and of this natural tendency, managers at all levels can be expected to allocate their time and efforts among needs on an individual, and different, basis *in the absence of some strong control to the contrary.* Among other things, this suggested planning process provides such a control.

Timing of the Business

The other aspect of time which ought to be assessed is the timing of the business as a whole in the service of particular needs. Although this may seem somewhat nebulous in concept, it is most practical, and often critical, in application.

George Romney undoubtedly attributes much of his success with

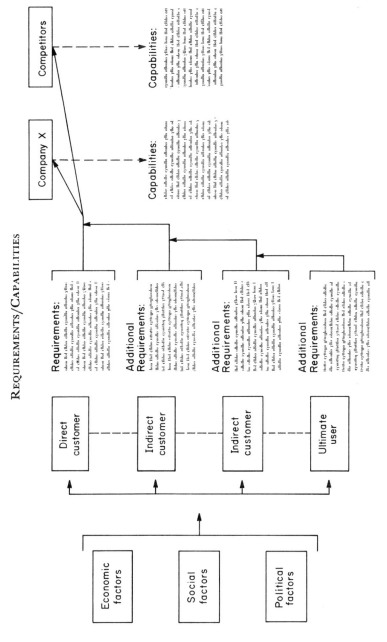

CHART VIII

REQUIREMENTS/CAPABILITIES

American Motors to the timing he used in promoting the compact car. Favorable or unfavorable timing is determined by many factors, but basically by economic, social, and political influences on needs, customers, and competition. Also, of course, it is materially affected by competition's appreciation of and response to these influences. Wouldn't the results have been different for the Rambler if the Big Three had not been asleep at the switch?

In some instances, the most favorable time for a particular business is after someone else has blazed the trail in serving a need in a new way. This is generally true when the business has limited financial resources and the new method of serving the need requires heavy expenditures for development or introduction.

TOTAL UNDERSTANDING

The understanding of resources provided by an analysis of this kind is necessary for sound decisions as to what should be done about a particular need. It is necessary in total with respect to all needs in which the business is interested; in fact, it is the only valid basis on which management can determine whether its resources are excessive or deficient, and to what extent those resources are being fully utilized in the service of customer needs.

In the absence of this total understanding, it is standard practice for management to dispose of some resources in times of crisis and cost cutting—only to turn around, even months later, and try to retrieve them. When they are manpower resources, as is too often the case, the lack of understanding is costly to the business indeed and sometimes fatal.

The examination of resources from the standpoint of their significance to customer needs, rather than their significance to anyone inside the business, is most revealing and rewarding. It tells what the business can count on in grappling with the future situation and what else may be required for success.

Chart VIII, "Requirements/Capabilities," depicts this evaluation of resources vis-à-vis situation. It summarizes some of the previous discussion and reveals the fundamental principles which we have seen are guides to sound business planning and operation.

General, but continuing and important, guidance for company planning is provided by the chosen area of operation (scope) and the timeless intentions of the business (purpose). Both are the responsibility of general management.

6. Scope and Purpose Of the Enterprise

OUGHT THE BUSINESS TO BE INTERESTED IN EXER-cising known capabilities in serving particular needs? This is the next question which the planner, continuing his work of introspection, must ask himself. It should be answered in the affirmative before he and others begin to develop ways of actually applying those capabilities. If general management has already decided what the specific area of operation should be, that decision will provide the answer, in whole or in part.

Abercrombie & Fitch is one company that has apparently faced up to this question and answered it profitably. To quote its president, John H. Ewing:

It has long been convenience to the nth degree for the housewife in suburbia or rural America to select her basic household needs . . . from a catalog and then simply mail an order blank. This kind of mail order selling is more than adequately handled by this country's leading volume mail order houses. . . . But there remains an area of need . . . which still requires time-consuming, fatiguing, and costly trips to town; i.e., the need for *luxury* items, *unusual* gift items, and *top-quality* accoutrements to living. The desire for luxury items is a desire quite common to all men. You'll find it is expressed occasionally by most people when they find themselves suddenly a bit more solvent than usual. On the other hand, it is expressed regularly by people who do have the means all the time. This latter group represents some 30 per cent of the American buying public! This is the prime market Abercrombie & Fitch directs its selling message to—we catalog everything from 35-cent leaders to $2,100 guns. We concentrate our merchandise in the area of sport and leisure—an important part of the life of those in this category—the . . . *affluent group*—those with a ready, open-to-buy frame of mind.[1]

SCOPE

At some point in time—the sooner the better—every business must choose its area of operation, which for easy reference has been termed *scope*. The obvious has already been noted: No business, not even the so-called giant, can operate in all areas. It cannot be all things to all people; it must be something to some people. Even so, one might argue that in view of the dynamics inherent in situation and resources, a business should not don a straitjacket in the form of a definite scope. However, this line of apparently plausible thought fails to recognize (1) the reason for determining a particular area of operation, (2) the correct means of doing so and stating the decisions thus reached, and (3) the proper use of scope in planning and conducting a business. The following comments and suggestions are directed to these interrelated aspects of the scope problem.

Boundary Marks for the Business

The stated scope of a business should define the limits, or boundary marks, within which it will operate. Such a delineation permits the business to start operations and prevents it from wasting time considering, or wasting time and resources engaging in, activities beyond the chosen area. A vague idea of scope may enable management to get started, but it is an open invitation to proliferation of thought and action in the future. Whatever the chosen area, all thought and action should be concentrated on it. This does not mean that the business must be blind to other areas and their possibilities. It does mean that interest in other areas is strictly secondary unless and until a conscious and careful management decision has been made to broaden scope.

L. T. Peifer, then executive vice president of the Brunswick Corporation's Sports Division, explained that company's thinking as follows:

[1] From "Catalog Selling Joins the Elite," a presentation at the Thirty-Fourth Annual Boston Conference on Distribution, 1962.

We at Brunswick . . . looked at our strengths and our weaknesses and determined what type of activities we were really good at. We concluded that we did not want to become one of the also-rans in the race for highly electronic and technical progress. We knew we were basically a recreational activity, and we channeled part of our future program in that direction. We also could read the projections and interpret the statistics as well as anybody. These indicated that leisure time was an important factor for the future. More paid vacations, less hours worked, more leisure for the new developing families. In addition, the booming population was certainly going to place particular emphasis on the growth in schools and hospitals [while] . . . studies of geriatrics and longevity indicated that the health field would be something that would fit in with our pattern as long as we did not become too technical and attempt to compete with the pharmaceutical companies. . . .

Our basic objective in the Business Development Program at Brunswick was to expand and diversify into newer, dynamic growth fields in the recreation, education, and health areas while at the same time [seeking] to maintain and strengthen the existing product structure of our company by acquiring new products, additional channels of distribution, and research and development activities that could have future profit possibilities. . . .[2]

Guides to Selection

How should a business choose its area of operation? First, it must recognize that the aim of scope is to define the area of *primary* interest. Second, it must appreciate the fact that it does not have complete freedom; its choice is limited by the peculiar capabilities which it has or can obtain. Third, management must realize that these capabilities have business usefulness only to the extent that they permit service of particular customer needs.

Only a very general or vague idea of scope is possible before the business has studied its situation and resources as described in Chapters 4 and 5. This process will reveal what the extreme limits of scope should be. There is no reason why any area should be included for which the company has no capability; in fact, as already indicated, there are reasons why any such area should *not* be included.

Management may decide either to define scope very broadly or to

[2] From "Growth Through a Positive Approach to Diversification," a presentation at the Thirty-Third Annual Boston Conference on Distribution, 1961.

limit activities to a more restricted area. For example, a mature business with relatively unlimited manpower and funds may choose the widest possible scope, while a new enterprise whose manpower and funds are still modest will often do well to be more restrictive—at least temporarily. To anticipate Chapter 8, a decision of the latter kind is a strategic decision by general management, reflecting its judgment that for the time being, in light of all the existing circumstances, it will be best for the business to concentrate on certain needs, for which it has capability, to the exclusion of others. Such a decision is a major one and most difficult. It cannot be made without knowledge, or a most unusual sort of intuition, concerning situation and resources.

Another common restriction on scope which should be recognized by management and possibly interpreted as a limiting factor is the basic nature of its capability. For example, one business may try to serve cooking needs with products developed through electrical technology. Another may be interested only in products using gas. The first may choose to offer only steel products, the second aluminum or glass or plastics. Management's decision to limit the area of business operation accordingly reflects not only an assessment of the business's capabilities but some understanding of how the situation will develop, particularly with respect to the relative success of one kind of technology or material over others in the service of particular needs.

In addition there is the geographical factor. Geography also restricts possible scope and should be considered by management. A business may be able to serve a need which is found not only in this country but, say, in the European Common Market. United States businesses of equal capability may reach different decisions as to whether ECM should be considered within their scope. These decisions can be critical and for soundness depend heavily upon an understanding of the developing situation.

This element of business planning, like all others, is directed to the future. The present and past are important only for the basis and perspective they provide for the future. Therefore, in identifying and evaluating resources as related to customer needs for "scoping," the business must project not only what is but what probably will be.

It should be obvious too that no definition of scope can be considered final in any sense until *all possible* customer needs have been carefully studied. In the ordinary course of events, a business should progressively gain a better understanding, and achieve a more precise definition, of its scope. Recognition of the necessity for an evolving definition and of the dynamics inherent in customer needs and resources should put to rest anyone's fear that the attempt to define scope exactly will put undesirable blinders on a business. And this fear can be fully dispelled, of course, by special, systematic attention to the possibilities of changing scope after it has been defined.

Crowdus Baker, president of Sears, Roebuck & Company, emphasizes the fact that "Sears' orientation is toward the future." The company must, he has said, continue to define its role in the broadest way possible.

> Sears must conceive of itself as a distributor rather than as a retailer—and the company must think of the future in terms of the customer rather than products. . . .
>
> Up until 1925, Sears was solely a mail order house. If the company had thought of itself as being . . . only in this field, inevitably we would have found ourselves limited by the mail order market. In an effort to keep up with the changing shopping patterns of our customers, we were forced to redefine our function—to become a system of distribution.[3]

A Clear Definition

Except for limited and special attention, the business should be devoting its time and efforts solely to the chosen area of operation. If this fundamental operating principle is recognized, and if the area is known with some exactness, the planner will not ordinarily in the steps previously described be examining customer needs which are outside scope. If he happens on a need, outside scope, which he believes holds great promise and should be evaluated, he or someone else will study it and make recommendations concerning it which may lead to a change in scope. If, however, scope is not precisely defined and known to the marketing planner, he may unwittingly spend most of his time in the study of needs which are outside the company's province or at least questionable on that score.

[3] From "After Seventy-Five Years—Looking Ahead," a presentation at the Thirty-Third Annual Boston Conference on Distribution, 1961.

The sequential consideration of scope after resources and situation is intended to narrow down further planning efforts to those which represent real opportunities for the business. If scope is to serve this end in the planning activity, it should be contained in a clear statement which will tell all concerned just which customer needs are included in the area of operation. If these needs have been properly determined, all will be needs which *could* be served by the business, but some of them may be needs which it is not at present serving. The inclusion of a particular need in scope implies a decision, not that the business *will* serve it, but only that management must be constantly aware of any opportunities which may stem from that need and of their relative importance to the profitable growth of the business. (Chart III, in Chapter 2, reflects this line of thinking and so may be worth another look here.)

A clear statement of scope, in other words, singles out particular needs from the universe of customer needs. As noted, it may also appropriately identify the resources to be employed in their service, if only certain kinds are to be used, as compared with the kinds used by others to serve the same needs. And, if there are to be any geographic limitations, they too should be spelled out.

Without a clear and complete definition of scope, some planning can be done, but it is not likely to lead to the most profitable growth possible. With it, each function will have a basic and continuing guide to the kind of resources to be developed and maintained and the direction of their future application.

Two possible statements of scope for our stove manufacturer follow:

1. The scope of the X Company shall be the service of customer needs for means of cooking food in the home.

   This scope has no limitations of geography or capabilities. It also covers all kinds of food cooking in the home: for example, roasting, baking, stewing, grilling, toasting bread, making waffles.

2. The scope of the Y Company shall be the service of customer needs within the United States for means of cooking food in the home, which can be served by products using any form of gas fuel.

   This scope has limitations of both geography and capabilities.

Both these statements are incomplete in that they fail to recognize expressly all the dynamics of resources and needs. This shortcoming can be corrected by adding the words " . . . and any other customer needs which can be served by utilization of the kind of resources available to the company." As unnamed needs are identified, they can and should be specified.

PURPOSE

If scope has been defined, the planner should have the whole answer to the question whether the business ought to be interested in serving certain perceived needs which are outside scope. What about needs which are *within* scope? With regard to these he has only a partial answer—"perhaps" or "maybe." To have a more complete answer, he must understand the *purpose* of the business.

Consideration of purpose completes the inside look at the business which began with a study of resources and proceeded with a review of scope. It is the third phase of the organization's self-analysis.

For reasons which have been expressed or implied, or which will be developed, it is essential that general management consciously, carefully, and clearly determine why it is in business. More often than not it ducks this issue or improvises from month to year— hoping, apparently, that the business will find itself. In some cases the business may and does, but at what cost and waste of opportunity?

This third phase of business self-analysis requires an understanding, and application to planning, of the basic, continuing purpose of the business which evolves from what we have called its timeless intentions.

The Profit Intention

Every person with the will to live intends to breathe. Every business intends to make a profit, for the simple reason that it cannot exist without profit.

This profit intention of the business finds tangible expression and measurement in several forms. There are short-term profits and long-term profits. There are profits by product, by line, and by division.

There are profits as measured by percentage of sales and percentage of investment. All have some usefulness in planning and operating the business; however, management cannot afford to become so preoccupied with these different yardsticks that it fails to emphasize, for all concerned, the underlying intention and its many implications. For example, short-term profits are desirable in themselves, but what about the long term? Similarly, a profit on one product is welcome, but possibly not at the expense of another, while a profit in one area may be necessary to offset a temporary loss elsewhere.

A business satisfies this timeless intention to make *some* profit and thereby survive only over the long term and as a whole. Profitability cannot be determined by a look at one point in time alone, or by the health of one segment of the business, or by one form of profit measurement.[4] Yet the need to make a profit is so basic that it is assumed, more than it is expressed, by businessmen. The objectives and hoped-for results of particular products and programs, as well as the short-term aspects of profit, receive most of the attention. Hence American business suffers both internally and externally.

Opponents of business may choose, for their own reasons, to ignore the timeless profit intention and its justification of specific profit results. Many others, however, either do not understand it at all or suffer from a complete misconception of the word "profit" and its meaning. Business would benefit in its relation with government and the public if the profit motive, with all its implications, were expressed and explained more often—not just when a particular business or industry is being pilloried for political or other reasons. Fortunately, some leaders not only are awake to this problem but are doing something about it. Fred C. Foy, Koppers' board chairman, urges:

> Let's not be like the political office-seeker who was so modest that he didn't vote for himself during the election—and lost by one vote. Let's cast our votes for our beliefs. Let's tell the American public that we want profits, because they need profits if we are to keep creating the jobs America will need as it continues to grow.[5]

[4] For a complete discussion of profits and the development of an economic approach to executive decisions, see Joel Dean, *Managerial Economics*, Prentice-Hall, Inc., New York, 1951.

[5] "Do We Know Enough—Talk Enough About Profits?" a presentation before the 55th Annual Meeting of the National Industrial Traffic League, Pittsburgh, November 1962.

Every business, in fact, will benefit internally as well as externally from a constant reminder that it cannot be interested in, or become involved with, matters that have no profit possibilities—and that it is most interested in those that have the greatest profit possibilities.

It is amazing how often experienced businessmen become so enamored with volume that they almost lose sight of profit. This sort of infatuation is most prevalent in larger companies where organization and procedures tend to remove many key people from close proximity to the realities of corporate survival and profit is treated as the responsibility of the financial group and perhaps the general manager. Is it any wonder, then, that others sometimes fail to recognize the profit implications of their actions? How can salesmen, for example, help but be volume-minded when all their performance standards and incentives are expressly or indirectly related to volume?

For initial guidance, the profit intention might be expressed most simply as follows: *to make—if not maximum profit—at least enough to assure continuing investor support.* A business cannot apply this measure too soon to any chance it sees to serve a customer need. If it offers no profit possibilities over the long term, management ordinarily should not be interested in it. The planner will therefore at this stage and time drop consideration of any such need. He will do so even though the business has the required capability and service if the need is within the declared scope of the business. If, on the other hand, there are apparent possibilities of profit, he will proceed with his evaluation, which will eventually lead to a definite determination of specific prospects.

Growth or Death

Every business has, in addition, a timeless intention concerning growth. It must respond to its environment, and that response must in essence be growth or death. The word "growth" is used here in its largest sense and does not necessarily imply growth in absolute terms. A company may propose to grow in total dollar sales within a certain geographic area and a certain field of interest, or to grow on a worldwide scale through diversification, or to grow in importance in a certain field without absolute growth in dollar volume.

The growth intention is inseparable from the profit intention.

They go hand in hand and have a reciprocating effect on one another. (This is the reason why reference is usually made to *"profitable* growth.") Together they form the basis for specific programs and objectives. The programs may not materialize, and kinds of growth other than those intended may result, if the nature of the company's intentions is not known and kept in mind by all concerned.

Whether a business is living up to its plans for growth can be determined only by looking at the long term. For any given short term, growth may be great, small, or nonexistent—or the business may even regress. The simplest and broadest statement of the growth intention might be *to grow within scope*—that is, if scope has been defined.

Knowledge of the growth intention is useful in the planning process primarily as an indicator of the relative importance to the business of its various chances to serve one or more needs. If one chance could lead to growth of a kind particularly favored, it should of course take precedence over others in further evaluation and recommendation.

Supporting Intentions

Every business should also have still further intentions, and many do. Most of these can be considered supporting intentions, included by implication in profitable growth because they concern timeless factors which affect it.

As one example, the future of any business rests for the most part, figuratively and literally, on the shoulders of its personnel: those now employed and those to be employed in later years. The full realization of their individual capabilities provides one of the strongest possible thrusts toward profitable growth. A company might therefore state its intention *to provide opportunity for full development of each individual in the business.*

In the same way the customer-oriented company might declare its intention *to gear all activities to the service of customer needs.* And, since it is increasingly recognized that the opinion of the public in general, not just customers, has a major impact on any firm, management might resolve *to build respect for the business with all segments of the public.*

When basic, timeless intentions such as these have been adopted, they prescribe the kinds of long-term results which the business should achieve. Both intentions and results desired, if known, provide general but continuing guidance for all the activities of the business.

Interpretation by General Management

The guidance to be derived from a statement of purpose is, in fact, so basic and general that it requires constant interpretation. The general manager has the responsibility and authority to interpret it as of, and for, any given time. If he fails to do so, he must expect the functional areas to make their own, possibly different or even conflicting, interpretations.

The general manager makes and communicates his interpretation in several ways. Whether he intends to or not, for example, he interprets the purpose of his business every time he makes a decision. Suppose he approves the pursuit of a certain opportunity which promises yearly profits amounting to 10 per cent of sales. In the absence of any express statement to the contrary, this decision declares that 10 per cent profit is sufficient to satisfy the company's intention *to make—if not maximum profit—at least enough to assure continuing investor support.*

Approval by a general manager of a major research and development program in a new field of technology can determine that the growth of the business shall take that direction and that the rate of growth must be accelerated even at the expense of immediate profit. General management decisions leading to personnel training programs and systematic job rotation interpret the intention *to provide opportunity for full development of each individual in the business.* Similarly, through participation in certain community affairs general management conveys its understanding of how best *to build respect for the business with all segments of the public.*

Importance of Written Statement

In short, even if the purpose of the business has not been expressed in so many words, it can be surmised from all general management

decisions and actions. If it has not been communicated to all concerned, both inside and outside the business, people can only conclude from observation and experience what timeless intentions are
to guide them. Their conclusions will be based on their observation,
not only of general management, but of anyone else in the business
with whom they have contact. Thus a written statement of purpose is
one means of minimizing the inevitable misunderstandings.

Here, however, our concern with purpose is with its bearing on
planning and general management decisions, not its contribution to
public relations. And a statement of purpose in written form is useful to the general manager in reaching decisions because it provides
him with a ready reference to the basic check points which must be
taken into consideration. At the same time it provides others in the
business with a common, accurate understanding of the timeless intentions which are guiding, and are being interpreted by, general
management decisions.

Even when purpose has been expressed in writing, people will
rightly or wrongly read interpretations of it into general management decisions and actions. Hence the general manager can and
should interpret purpose in a more formal, less piecemeal fashion
through the development and issuance of statements of policy concerning its every aspect. This practice forces the manager, and those
who assist him in the development of these policy statements, to
think carefully. It results in the fuller understanding which in turn
helps the manager to apply more consistent judgment to individual
decisions.

Statements of policy should be reviewed at least annually and
modified whenever required by any change in general management's
interpretation of purpose.

*   *   *

Thus, at this point in the planning process, management's
thoughts are turning to what future action might be taken by the
business with respect to the needs, customers, and competition identified in situation.

- Future action *should be influenced* by anticipated customer
  action and competitive action.

- Future action *will be permitted or limited* by the capabilities implied by resources.
- Future action *ought to be directed generally* by the kinds of results the business intends to achieve over the long term.

There are many kinds of results in which a business may be interested; they range from financial to personnel, from short-term to long-term. The company should get its primary guidance or bearing from the kinds of results which are considered to be most important to it. Long-term results are always more important than short-term; and profitable growth, because of the nature of any business and its basic responsibility to society, is the most important result to be achieved and, therefore, the most important timeless intention.

In summary, then, this is the purpose of the business.

The basic frame of reference for business planning must be provided by marketing. There is a prescribed sequence for its refinement and use by research, engineering, manufacturing, finance, and general management; and planning within each of these areas of specialization bears a definite relationship to planning for the business as a whole.

7. Opportunities and Their Evaluation

THE PLANNER SHOULD NOW BE GAZING UPON HIS Land of Opportunity. He should know its location, dimensions, and principal characteristics. But he has decisions to make about what, when, and how the business will inhabit and cultivate this Land of Opportunity. Everything cannot be considered and decided at once. Matters must be handled one at a time, in an orderly fashion, if the best decisions are to be reached. This orderliness can be partly achieved by continuing to consider each need separately. It will not be fully achieved, however, unless the business (1) examines and makes a decision about each different chance it has to serve any needs and (2) relates all chances and decisions to one another.

We have said over and over that if a business is unable to serve a particular need, that need holds no opportunities for that particular business. It may hold opportunities for others. If a business does have the necessary capabilities, it has at least one chance to serve the need and, hence, an opportunity. If it can serve the need through basically different resources, it has more than one chance and, therefore, more than one opportunity. In the latter case, each chance or opportunity will involve different actions, different results, and possibly may even conflict with the others. Therefore, throughout the balance of our discussion, needs will be considered in terms of the specific opportunity or opportunities they represent. This shifting of focus is still another illustration of the "narrowing down" force which is built into this business planning process.

The planner may choose to consider a particular need as offering several different chances and opportunities even though the same, rather than different, resources are used in its service. This is most desirable when substantially different classes of direct customers are involved—although exactly the same product may be offered to each. For example, a manufacturer of small electrical motors may sell the same item to appliance manufacturers and to toy makers. Each class of customer represents an opportunity. This approach is most desirable; also, if only one class of direct customer is involved but even slightly different products are offered them, opportunities will then be related to the different products. For example, the electric motor manufacturer may offer appliance manufacturers his standard motor with and without a built-in automatic cutoff, which gives him two opportunities to serve appliance manufacturers.

The planner should identify separate chances from the standpoint of their significance to the business. Suppose the business is serving only one need and has five direct customers. The planner may in this event choose to consider each customer as a separate opportunity. This is helpful if for some reason internal to the business each should be considered separately and decisions ought to be made, and action planned, on an individual basis. Otherwise, it makes for duplication of effort.

In this step of business planning, the planner aims to describe in meaningful terms all the individual opportunities arising from situation. This is, however, only preliminary to recommendations on the part of the planner as to what should be done about each opportunity, when, and how. These recommendations are reviewed, and cumulatively amended or confirmed, by all functions of the business and, finally, by general management.

MARKETING'S RESPONSIBILITY

Thus far the marketing planner has been carrying the ball. He must now, to repeat, take one more important step before he can pass the ball to his associates in the other functions of the business. He must complete his own analysis of each opportunity separately and decide what, in his opinion, should be done about it. He must do this in a manner which will be helpful to marketing and all the other functions as they consider his recommendations and, after these have been approved or modified, as they take the necessary action.

Basic Frame of Reference

In other words, it is the responsibility of the marketing function to provide the basic frame of reference for the consideration of all the opportunities available to the business. This is a grave obligation, not to be taken lightly.

> The best way to avoid ending up in an overcrowded and overly competitive situation, according to Celanese's Chairman Harold Blancke, is to be among the first to detect and develop new market opportunities. Celanese's management could take pride in its achievements on this score. About ten years ago it saw that the growth and profits of Celanese's old-line acetate and rayon fibers were on the wane. The company then boldly set out to upgrade its basic know-how in cellulose polymers into more sophisticated and profitable products such as nytril fibers, polyethylene and polyesters. In 1962 the protracted, and often painful, push into these products finally came to full flower. Strongly helped by a sales boom in textile fibers as well as in chemicals, volume jumped 15.1 per cent to $238.1 million for the nine months, while net soared 60.6 per cent to a record of $20.1 million.[1]

Obviously, so far-reaching a responsibility should neither be assigned nor accepted without a clear understanding of its many implications.

First of all, if a business adopts this approach to business planning, it is consciously or otherwise reaching certain conclusions and adopting the position that, in addition to the accepted financial, manufacturing, engineering, and research activities, it needs a function which can provide the framework within which decisions can be made as to what kind of product will be offered for sale, to whom, where, when, and how. This function will be responsible for knowing all that the business must know about customer needs, customers, and competition. Any such knowledge gained through the other functions is merely an extra dividend. Any lack of it will be the sole responsibility of this one group.

[1] "Chemicals," *Forbes,* January 1, 1963, p. 68.

The function will also be responsible for identifying all chances that the business will have to serve customer needs within the limitations of its resources, scope, and purpose. If other functions aid in the identification of opportunities, so much the better, but any shortcomings in identification will be the sole responsibility of this one, which will further be charged with first recommending what opportunities should be pursued by the business, when, how, and with what probable results. Its recommendations must be based on the demands of the marketplace, but must take into account the business's known resources and, again, its scope and purpose.

This new function will be responsible for planning and executing any sales programs, together with any supporting programs (such as advertising and sales promotion) which are appropriate to the pursuit of opportunities, in the manner finally determined or approved by general management. This new function might, in fact, appropriately be called—and generally *is* called—the marketing function.

Evaluation of Individual Opportunities

We assume, then, that our planner is in marketing. How does he go about providing the basic frame of reference for the consideration of all opportunities by all functions of the business?

He first sets aside any opportunity which does not deserve further evaluation. Ordinarily this initial screening should eliminate only those opportunities which relate to needs of insignificant future magnitude and which are not otherwise important to the business. However, great care should be taken to avoid setting aside opportunities which are small but are importantly connected with large needs. They may be small only because near-term technology appears to be limiting—as in the case of the stove manufacturer whose opportunity to serve cooking needs through electronic ranges currently may be very small, although it would be a serious mistake for him not to evaluate it from the standpoint of all functions with an eye to the future. The general manager may decide not to pursue such an opportunity now, but this decision should not be made until after he has heard from all functions.

All opportunities remaining after this initial screening should be evaluated individually by marketing. This first evaluation is aimed at determining what volume and market position, over the planning period, could be obtained if the business chose to pursue each opportunity *alone*. It should reflect anticipated plans and actions of customers, anticipated plans and actions of competitors, knowledge of the different courses of action which the business could take in matching or beating competition, and marketing judgment concerning these possible courses of action.

A record should be made of marketing's evaluation in a form meaningful, not only to marketing, but to all the other functions and to general management. Its nature is indicated by the following review of the points to be covered. It might be headed "Marketing Data for Opportunity No. 1."

1. *Identification of the opportunity.* The report begins with a summary description of the need involved and the chance to serve it in terms of class of customers, kind of resource, or whatever is most significant to the business.

2. *Magnitude, timing, and proposed participation in opportunity.* A historic record should cover whatever period is significant and represented by available data. A projection of the future should cover the planning period, by 12-month intervals, for at least five years. For example:

	Historic Record				*Current Year*	*Future for Planning Period*			
	1950	*1955*	*1960*	*1964*	*1965*	*1966*	*1967*	*1968*	*1969*
Need									
(units or $)	100	200	300	350	400	500	600	700	800
Opportunity									
(units or $)	100	200	200	250	300	300	400	500	600
Proposed volume									
(units or $)	50	100	100	100	100	150	200	250	300
Market position:									
% to need	50	50	33	28	25	30	33	36	31
% to opportunity	50	50	50	40	33	50	50	50	50

Since all projections are expressions of judgment, it must be recognized by everyone, not just the function preparing them, that they indicate magnitude and timing *generally*. They could probably be more accurate if stated in terms of range, but range projections are awkward to handle in many cases. Rather, the simplest possible form should be used in view of the data's intended use—guidance in evaluation and planning. If the range of either magnitude or time is relatively large and is likely to be particularly significant to any function of the business, that range should be shown in some manner. The rule-of-thumb test for such significance is: Will knowledge of the range materially affect proposals concerning this opportunity? For example, projections of its size and timing may depend substantially upon a judgment concerning technological progress in developing a material. If a breakthrough should be made within one year rather than two as anticipated, volume could increase a year earlier and possibly—because of timing—the increase could be much greater than projected.

Every effort should be made, however, to avoid cluttering up projections with mere hedges against inaccuracy. They are not offered, and should not be used, as accurate forecasts. They are merely indicative and will be more meaningful to all concerned if the principal factors used in their determination are known, recorded, and communicated. These factors might appropriately take the form of critical conclusions and assumptions. They can be stated in any form, and at random, but they can be more easily identified (and their significance more clearly understood) if they are organized around the three keys to situation—needs, customers, and competition—and what the business can do about them.

3. *Critical conclusions and assumptions concerning needs.* The first and by far the most important conclusion is that the business is trying to serve Need *X*, not Need *Y*. As noted, confusion on this point misdirects all planning and all action; therefore, the product and service requirements of Need *X* must be stated or summarized. These requirements provide the basis for (1) assumptions as to the direction which product improvements by competition will take and (2) conclusions as to the proper direction for the business's own improvements. In other words, they are the practical ideal.

The projected volume and timing of an opportunity must reflect judgments concerning what is now being done, and what can be done in the future, to meet certain of these requirements. If the nature or extent of an improvement in performance is critical, any conclusion or assumption concerning it should be noted as it relates to projected volume. And, if the proposed volume turns primarily on the anticipated availability of a new product by a certain date, any assumptions as to kind of product and date of availability should be stated and communicated to all concerned. The proposed volume shown by the tabulation on page 107, it will be noted, calls for a 50 per cent increase in 1966. This is dependent upon the availability during the first quarter of a substantially improved product in comparison with what has been offered in past years.

In brief, if the business's situation is fully understood, and if resources have been carefully evaluated within the limitations of scope and purpose, clues to the conclusions and assumptions to be organized under this heading have already been spread out on the table in front of the planner.

4. *Critical conclusions and assumptions concerning customers.* In Chapter 4 we saw how the magnitude of needs is affected by the numbers of direct and indirect customers and the economic, social, and political environment in which they will exist in the future. Conclusions and assumptions concerning major developments in these areas are no less critical than others, and the magnitude and timing of opportunities are similarly affected. For example, continued or accelerated trends toward more convenient living and toward a greater proportion of working wives and mothers may foretell new and rapidly growing opportunities for some businesses.

Changes—if of major dimensions—in the location of customers could affect the size of opportunities and most certainly will affect the way in which a business should seek to obtain its proposed volume. Anticipated population increases in Florida and on the West Coast now are important planning factors for companies directly serving consumer needs and for suppliers of those companies.

It is obvious, too, that the nature and probable solution of customers' operating problems, if those customers are other businesses, can affect the magnitude and timing of opportunities and of the volume which the business should expect to obtain from them. The progress of automation in plants of a certain class could, among other factors, well be critical.

Again, if the situation is fully understood, a basis will have been found for conclusions and assumptions which should be recorded and communicated as appropriate.

5. *Critical conclusions and assumptions concerning competition.* No one knows what competition is actually going to do—not even competition. Anticipation of competitive action with respect to cus-

tomers and to product and service requirements is, however, always critical in projecting the magnitude and timing of an opportunity and of the volume the business should seek to obtain. These projections, particularly the more important ones, cannot be used to guide counteraction if they are not properly identified and communicated.

A business must to some extent tip its hand regarding most planned action of major consequence. Its intentions can generally be inferred from available information concerning new factories, new basic materials, new organizational setups, or financial strength. Intelligent observation and analysis of published data are likely to be more productive and reliable than activities which might be described as industrial espionage. Some businesses do take the trouble, for instance, to study the annual reports of their competitors. Whether they are organized to analyze and utilize the information to be found there is another matter.

In any case, there is ample raw material for reasonable conclusions and assumptions concerning future competitive action. All that the planner needs to do at this stage is to record them and communicate at least the most important of them.

Recording all conclusions and assumptions concerning needs, customers, and competition is one way of forcing the closest possible scrutiny of their probable individual and collective impact. Communicating them throughout the business has several desirable end results: It provides everyone with a basic understanding of the all-important marketplace; it gives all interested parties the more important facts and reasoning supporting the planner's recommendations; and it permits constructive amplification or modification of conclusions and assumptions on the basis of additional facts or superior judgment in any and all areas of the business.

6. *Special marketing action programs and marketing's viewpoint on the impact of opportunity.* The data suggested under Headings 1 through 5 provide the basic frame of reference for the consideration of each opportunity by everyone interested. Of less direct interest to many others in the business are the action programs within the marketing function which are designed to support the recommendations of the planner. He should, however (provided he is in marketing), include in his record and communications an outline of any special marketing programs required and tentatively planned. This

should cover whatever the other functional areas need to know in order to support them with their own programs. Enough information should also be provided to permit (1) finance to estimate the marketing costs of serving the opportunity, (2) general management to understand marketing's part in the total action program to be developed, and (3) general management to know marketing's opinion concerning the importance to the business of pursuing the opportunity as recommended.

To this end, the marketing planner should record and communicate:

a. A general description of any special marketing programs required.
b. A summary statement of any additional marketing resources required.
c. An estimate of the marketing time, effort, and cost involved.
d. A proposal concerning strategy.
e. An estimate of the calculated risk from a marketing standpoint.
f. A summary of the cumulative effect which pursuit of the opportunity, as recommended, will have on
  (1) Previously planned and scheduled marketing work on other opportunities.
  (2) Previously evaluated opportunities still under consideration by the business.
  (3) Important marketing resources.
g. Marketing's opinion as to whether the proposed pursuit of this opportunity is consistent with the purpose of the business and what contribution it will make to stated overall objectives.

The kind of record and communication suggested under this last heading will set a pattern to be followed by all the other functions in their subsequent evaluations.

Pursuit of the opportunity, as recommended, may call for very little special effort by the marketing function. This will be the case if it involves a new product only slightly different from the one currently being sold and if it involves only the same customers. On the other hand, if it is a question of a new product and new customers, substantial additional marketing effort will be required, conceivably including the relocation and addition of field personnel, advertising and promotion to introduce the product, the establishment of field inventories, the training and placement of special product service personnel, and marketing research to test reaction to the product. These and other programs must be spelled out in detail within the marketing function to assure that they are properly planned and then, after approval by management, executed.

FUNCTIONAL PLANNING

If the marketing function has all these responsibilities, it has a dual planning role. Its contribution to overall planning for the business has been described in some detail in this and previous chapters. This role of "lead dog" is substantially completed with the evaluation of opportunities. Marketing's second role, however, concerns functional rather than overall company planning. It requires marketing planning which is similar in intent to research planning, engineering planning, manufacturing planning, and financial planning.

What are the nature and aim of functional planning? Planning in each functional area of the business involves the same kind of activities as are required for general planning. Each function must gather information, relate and express the pieces of information in a meaningful manner, develop recommendations and obtain management decisions on alternatives, and record the output of all these activities to guide and measure performance and to serve as a basis for future planning in that function. But each assumes a very different viewpoint in its planning activities, which concern very different kinds of skills and performance. The differences in viewpoint, skills, and performance are forces which, unless controlled, will drive the planning in these respective functional areas in opposite directions.

Coordination and Integration

If the planning in the functional areas is to be coordinated—or, better yet, integrated—a force greater than any of those mentioned must be found and used to bring them together. This integrative force is available. It consists of the opportunities of the business as a whole for profitable growth. If all planning revolves around this common axis or focal point, the differences in viewpoint, skills, and performance change from potential business liabilities to dynamic business assets.

Since planning, business or functional, is a continuous process, it can be accurately depicted by a circle as shown in Charts IV (p. 50), V (p. 51), and VI (p. 53). Therefore, the planning which takes place in each function might be represented by a separate circle. The trick is to get them all revolving around a single axis. To achieve this without duplication of effort, yet with full utilization of all the different viewpoints, skills, and activities of the different functions, marketing must form the axis initially. Marketing, more than any other function of the business, knows where to find the necessary material and how to shape it. But, after the axis has been formed by marketing, it must be forged and tempered by the other functions and by general management before it can fully do its job. [See Chart IV (p. 50), Chart V (p. 51), and Chart VI (p. 53).]

As marketing forms this axis, it is simultaneously planning what can and should be done in the marketing function. In the same way, as the other functions forge and temper it, they plan what can and should be done in their respective areas. Marketing reaches conclusions and makes assumptions concerning needs, customers, and competition. These are refined as the axis is forged and tempered. Marketing also reaches conclusions and makes assumptions concerning what could and should be done within the business about opportunities. These conclusions and assumptions are similarly refined.

This tempering process is continuous, just as planning in each function and for the business as a whole is continuous. Planning in one area should feed on planning in all others—and it will *if the business has basic planning procedures which permit or force cross-communication of essential matters.*

Marketing, it will be remembered, records and communicates data and judgments for the basic frame of reference outlined earlier in this chapter. Marketing should also, for its use in marketing planning, record appropriate data and judgments. The result might, for convenience, be called a "Statement of Marketing Planning." Since one reason for preparing it is to avoid the necessity for gathering and organizing the same information again at a later date, this statement should include all the data obtained by marketing on situation and resources. For ready use in the continuous planning activity, the

latest statements of scope and of purpose also should be included. To
them should be added all the material outlined under the six headings given on pages 107-111, together with the detailed information
from which it is drawn.

Sequence of Functional Evaluation

When marketing has completed its evaluation of each opportunity
and is ready to communicate it in the suggested form, to whom
should the ball be passed?

It should not be passed to the general manager because he wants
the cumulative data, judgment, and recommendations of all functional areas as the basis for his decisions. Nor should it be passed to
finance; costs and profits cannot be calculated, and cash flow and
other financial requirements cannot be planned, without a knowledge of proposed programs and anticipated results in all functional
areas. Manufacturing cannot receive the ball because production and
manufacturing facilities cannot be planned without a knowledge of
how and when products desired by marketing will be developed and
engineered. And engineering cannot take over if the desired product
must be developed by research.

The logical pass receiver, then, is research. Even if marketing has
not indicated that a new product will have to be developed by research, it is advisable to have the second evaluation made by this
function. The frame of reference provided by marketing will often
prompt an alert research function to suggest a product innovation
previously considered impossible—or one that was overlooked—and
any such suggestions should be fed into everyone's evaluation as soon
as possible.

No function should be a passive recipient of the basic frame of
reference from marketing, particularly not research or engineering.

Research evaluation. Upon receipt of "marketing data," research
evaluates each opportunity from its own viewpoint but within the
basic frame of reference. If, in the course of evaluation, any question
is raised concerning possible modification of the frame of reference,
it should be settled by consultation with the marketing planner. For
example, the magnitude of the need and that of the opportunity may
both depend heavily upon the extent and timing of technological

progress in a certain field by all industry. The thinking of research (and engineering) in this respect certainly should be most valuable to the business and reflected in the frame of reference. And, of course, if the proposed volume is related to a critical conclusion about a development by research, this conclusion must be confirmed by research or changed. In the latter event, the marketing planner must reconsider the proposed volume and any marketing programs which will be affected.

Research records and communicates the results of this second evaluation of each opportunity in a form similar to that used by marketing. It is not necessary for research to re-identify the opportunity or to restate magnitude, timing, and proposed participation, since any changes here have already been reflected by modifications in the "Marketing Data." Nor, for similar reasons, is it necessary for research to restate critical conclusions and assumptions. However, research should record and communicate any special research action programs and research's views on the impact of the opportunity. The "Research Data" record should parallel that of marketing as outlined under Section 6 of "Marketing Data" (pp. 110-111).

Like marketing, research has a dual planning role. It participates in and contributes to business planning, using and helping to refine the basic frame of reference initiated by marketing. But research must also be planning what supporting research activities must be carried on, when, how, and with what results. The record of this supporting planning, in the complete detail required for use in the supervision and control of research activities and as the base for the function's future planning, might be called a "Statement of Research Planning."

In the course of the evaluation by research, the possibility of another opportunity connected with the same or a different need may appear. Obviously, research should call this possibility to the attention of the marketing planner, and he should start its evaluation. If it proves to be an opportunity, it should be reviewed and evaluated by all concerned.

Engineering evaluation. When research has completed its evaluation, the ball is passed to engineering. This function, too, has a dual planning role. It participates in and contributes to overall planning, using the basic frame of reference initiated by marketing and sharpened by research, and it must also be planning what supporting engineering activities must be carried on, when, how, and with what results. The detailed record of this supporting planning might be called a "Statement of Engineering Planning."

Like research, the function of engineering can offer information and judgments which will lead to important refinements of the basic frame of reference. For example, its knowledge of engineering trends and progress in certain industries, or of particular customers or competitors, may prompt revisions in the estimated magnitude and timing of the opportunity. Such knowledge could easily suggest a change in the action proposed by marketing and research and should therefore be brought to the attention of those functions. Also, engineering may be able to make available for production a different kind of item than was anticipated, or it may propose an earlier or later date than was assumed by marketing. Any such circumstance should prompt at least a reconsideration by marketing of the proposed volume and of the critical conclusions and assumptions upon which that volume was predicated.

Whenever, in the course of engineering's evaluation, anything at all is developed which might change the basic frame of reference, that matter should be referred back to the marketing planner. After the required modification, the evaluation process begins anew. And, upon completion of this third evaluation, engineering records and communicates the results in statements similar to those prepared by research and marketing: "Engineering Data" and a "Statement of Engineering Planning."

Manufacturing evaluation. Manufacturing, like these other functions, has a dual planning role which it performs simultaneously. Similarly, too, manufacturing knowledge and judgment concerning trends and developments in certain industries, or of particular customers or competitors, may suggest modifications in the basic frame of reference for company planning which may affect the magnitude and timing of the opportunity. For example, the ability of manufacturing to produce more or less of a product than anticipated by marketing, or at one location but not at another, or at substantially lower or higher costs than planned, will certainly require amendment of the proposed volume.

Again, anything developed in the course of manufacturing evaluation which might require modification in the basic frame of reference is referred back to the marketing planner. After appropriate changes in the "Marketing Data," the opportunity is submitted for re-evaluation by research, engineering, and manufacturing.

Upon completion of its evaluation, manufacturing records and communicates the results of its thinking and planning as "Manufacturing Data." It should also record in detail what manufacturing activities must be carried on—when, how, and with what results—to support the overall planning. This "Statement of Manufacturing Planning" is useful for supervising and controlling manufacturing performance and planning future manufacturing activities.

Finance evaluation. The finance function has its own dual planning role and performs it in the same general manner as the other functions. Its knowledge and judgment concerning financial trends and developments may affect the magnitude or timing of the opportunity and thereby reshape the basic frame of reference. Ability or inability to finance certain facilities or programs may prompt revision of proposed action in any or all areas of the business. Finance also makes a unique contribution to the business's planning. It consolidates the special and ordinary expenses anticipated by all the other functions and estimates the profits and other financial results to be expected from their cumulative recommendations. Information of this kind can and should lead to possible changes not only in the basic frame of reference but in the planned activities of any or all functions. For example, if the profit possibilities of the opportunity being evaluated are revealed to be nonexistent, marketing will probably withdraw its original proposal. Or, if a reasonable profit seems possible only if new manufacturing facilities are provided, marketing may revise the proposed volume downward until construction can be completed. In any event, a poor profit picture should prompt every function to consider what can be done in its particular area to improve matters—both by cost reduction and by added value.

For most meaningful future reference, the summary of profit information developed by finance should be incorporated into the "Marketing Data" along with the details of magnitude, timing, and proposed participation (pp. 107-108). Profit in absolute dollars, as a per cent of sales and otherwise, will then be shown historically and for the future according to the volumes proposed.

In all other respects finance should record and communicate the results of its thinking and planning in the manner previously described; that is, as "Finance Data" and a "Statement of Financial Planning." The latter should cover detailed programing for use in supervising and controlling financial activities and in future planning.

THE ROLE OF THE GENERAL MANAGER

After the basic frame of reference has been modified as required by circumstances, and after the opportunity has been re-evaluated by all the individual functions, the cumulative recommendations as to that single opportunity are ready for consideration and decision by general management. What does the general manager have before him, what more does he require, and what should he do at this point in the planning process?

Cumulative Information and Recommendations

From the "Marketing Data" he can determine the nature, magnitude, and timing of the opportunity (pp. 107-108). The past record provides him with a certain perspective on the future, and additional insight is provided by comparison with the nature, magnitude, and timing of the need. He can quickly see whether the opportunity is growing or shrinking in size and how rapidly—in absolute terms and as related to the need, both of which are important.

The general manager knows the projected dimensions of both the opportunity and the need are not accurate, but he can have confidence in their general validity because they reflect the combined judgment of all the functional skills in his business after careful and systematic consideration of all available information. He can strengthen his confidence by referring to the critical conclusions and assumptions in the "Marketing Data," which now reflect the information and thinking, not just of the marketing people who initially prepared and recorded them, but of all the other functions as well. On the basis of this review and of his own information and judgment, the general manager may decide some of these dimensions should be verified by further study and possibly modified.

From the "Marketing Data," also, the general manager can determine what sales volume should be obtained in future years if the courses of action recommended by the functional areas are approved and carried out. He knows these volume projections are not accurate, but again he can have confidence in their general validity because they reflect combined judgment and integrated programing, and he can strengthen his confidence by referring to the critical conclusions and assumptions in the "Marketing Data" and to the special action programs of each function.

He can tell at a glance what the position of the business has been, and will be, relative to all competition (see pp. 109-110). The market-position data on percentage to opportunity show how the business stacks up against competitors who are trying to serve the same need through *similar means*. The data on percentage to need show how it compares with competitors who are using *any and all means*. This double approach to market position is designed to prevent any dangerous preoccupation with one's own capabilities. For example, the general manager may observe that the percentage to opportunity has been steadily increasing over the past few years and that the trend is expected to continue over the next five years. He will be encouraged by this fact alone. But, if he also observes that the percentage to need is declining, or at least not increasing, he will realize that other opportunities which impinge on this one are growing at its expense. In other words, his company's way of serving the need is proving less satisfactory to customers than the means of which others are capable.

Manufacturers of tin containers have recently faced this problem in extreme. Those who were serving the need for means of containing household amounts of detergents suddenly woke up to the fact that the use of tin was crumbling as a result of the growth of plastics. A manufacturer could be increasing his market position with respect to tin containers (percentage to opportunity) but be clinging to a market soon to be nonexistent. The switch from tin containers to blown plastic bottles for household detergents is now virtually complete after less than two years' competition from the substitute product.

When the general manager looks at the proposed volume, as related to the opportunity and the need, he may not be satisfied with the progress which is reflected. Assume, for example, that the opportunity is growing about 10 per cent a year, but the proposed volume shows a growth rate of 5 per cent. It is not enough to decide that the volume must be increased to obtain at least a 10 per cent growth. The general manager must also be willing to approve some changes in the proposed action programs which will assure that increase. It is his prerogative and responsibility to make his organization "stretch," but only on a realistic basis.

It is not uncommon for a general manager to take a projection of future volume, increase it by some arbitrary amount, and say: "We must get it in some way without any increase in expense." If that projection were prepared on the basis used in many businesses today, the general manager could be right just as easily as wrong in his decision. In effect, he is saying: "I do not believe the projection and will make my own." He has more than an even chance of being generally right—human nature being what it is and projections or forecasts what they are in most businesses.

However, if the proposed volume is developed through the cumulative information, thinking, and judgment of all the functions, and is supported by proposed action programs in each area, the general manager cannot make such an intuitive decision and expect it to work out. If he wants to increase the volume, he must expect and approve some change in the supporting programs. This will be a major change, if all the functions have done their planning carefully, because the originally proposed volume should be the best that can be expected with existing capabilities.

Instead of making an arbitrary decision to increase the proposed volume, the general manager should inquire what would be necessary in order to plan for a specified increase. It might be acceleration of an engineering project by added manpower or the addition of production facilities or field sales personnel. After the answer has been determined by reprocessing the cumulative recommendations of all the functions, an intelligent decision can be made. The general manager may decide to proceed as originally proposed, there being no possibility of increasing the volume, or he may decide to attempt an increase by assuming the risk and expense of major changes in the programs of several functional areas.

Volume should never be considered alone by anyone in the business, particularly the general manager. It must always be evaluated for profitability. A business lives on profit, not volume. Volume is important only as the vehicle for profit.

The information developed by finance tells the general manager what can be expected profitwise from the cumulative recommendations. Again, he may properly be dissatisfied with the projected results. But, again, he cannot make a "top of the head" or "seat of the pants" decision if he is using this planning process. Instead, he should inquire: "What expenses could be cut without changing the proposed volume and supporting programs, and at what risk? What expenses could be cut which would adversely affect volume, to what extent and at what risk? And what action—not now planned—could be taken which would build more customer value into the product and permit higher prices?"

Decision Making and Leadership

After the answers to these questions have been determined, the general manager can reach a sound decision. He can decide to accept those changes in supporting programs which will improve profit prospects, both short- and long-term. This will probably involve some effort to build more customer value into the product. He may choose to live temporarily with less profit than he wants in order to build a base for greater future profit. Or he may be forced by circumstances to achieve greater immediate profit at the possible expense of future profit. But at least he knows the nature of the risk and has a chance to do something about it. A decision on such a basis is a great deal different, in nature and consequence, from the customary panic decision to cut costs a given percentage "across the board."

General managers who are forced to make the latter type of decision should not be condemned. They should be pitied. They have no choice; they have not been given information, thinking, and recommendations which permit them to make discriminating judgments. Indeed, their very performance as leaders is threatened.

Ralph R. Brubaker, vice-president–marketing for the Carnation Company, has said:

I once heard the term "leader" defined as "a man who decides—sometimes he decides right, but *always* he decides!" If that definition has merit, it clearly implies that, to provide leadership to other people, an individual must be capable of making decisions.

It also implies the possibility of wide variation in the *quality* of decisions made and, in turn, of leadership provided. Even more important, it strongly suggests that leadership can be inadequate as well as adequate—that it can *deteriorate*, as well as improve or remain static. . . .

[The top executive] must not only be promptly and intimately aware of basic trends in the socio-economic area, in population needs, in distribution, in competition, and in government—he must also lead in initiating policy and program adjustments designed to exploit those trends or defend against them—and, most important of all, before the horse is out of the barn.[2]

The general manager is concerned with the major elements of the proposed action programs in each functional area and their integration with one another. He may properly question the magnitude or timing of these special programs and decide on changes which will reduce the risks involved. But these changes should be made only after reprocessing the possibilities through the entire evaluation system. Moreover, the general manager should not allow himself to be drawn into the details of proposed activities in any functional area—otherwise he will have neither the time nor the perspective to do his own job. Of course, a general manager must on occasion "dig into" functional areas of his business. This, however, should be by way of corrective supervision, not standard procedure.

The planning process assumes that no general manager can know everything about his business; that he expects those in each functional area to know more about their specialty than he knows; and that he is going to rely heavily upon their knowledge and abilities, when they are utilized in an organized and integrated manner, within the limitations of established scope and purpose. He should expect, require, and lean heavily on the evaluation by each function of the specific contribution it can and should make to the common cause. He should also require, and carefully weigh, its thinking concerning the course to be followed by the business as a whole; therefore, the outlined form for functional data calls for suggestions or proposals on strategy. (See Chapter 8.)

[2] From an address before the National Industrial Conference Board's 10th Annual Marketing Conference, September 20, 1962.

One Opportunity Versus Another

Our explanation of this opportunities element in business planning has concerned the procedure applicable to the evaluation of single opportunities, each considered alone. This explanation is so offered because, as a practical matter, the information concerning opportunities must be developed separately, no matter how much overlap or parallel there may be between them. However, a business must know all the opportunities available to it and should not decide what should be done about any one of them without knowing what it should do about all the rest.

Some opportunities impinge on others. Furthermore, a business may have the capabilities required to pursue a dozen opportunities, but it may not have enough—quantitywise—to pursue all of them. Even in the unlikely event that it can do so, it is improbable that management will or should pursue each with the same emphasis and effort. In theory, therefore, the final decision by the general manager on any one opportunity should not be made until all have been "racked up" before him, each with the cumulative recommendations of all the functional areas.

In time, with continuous planning, a business can approximate this perfect state. It will never attain it fully because new opportunities are continually arising from the dynamic situation and ever-changing resources. Even old opportunities are constantly changing for the same reasons.

The problem is most acute when the planning process is first applied. The general manager has before him Opportunity No. 1. "Marketing Data," "Research Data," "Engineering Data," "Manufacturing Data," and "Financial Data" most likely provide him with more complete information than he has ever had before concerning the separate functions of his business. If their cumulative recommendations are favorable and if, in the judgment of the general manager, they are sound, it would seem that a decision should be made to go ahead as planned. The general manager may feel, however, that he doesn't want to commit all the required resources to this particular opportunity until he knows as much about all the others. This can happen, for example, if the business has been running near capacity and the first opportunity is found to be much more promising, and the proposed volume greater, than was realized.

Under these circumstances, the general manager should in most cases still give his approval and direct that everyone proceed to carry out the recommendations.

Advancing the Time for Decisions

The wisdom of making, rather than reserving, decisions is clear if one takes into consideration that planning, by its nature, is a continuous thing. Studious effort is made throughout this book to avoid the noun "plan" because of its possible implications of finality. For the same reason, the word "planning" is emphasized. For, if planning is not recognized and practiced as a continuous thing, it can do as much harm as good to the business. That a business cannot be locked in a plan is a fact of business life. Some "hard-headed" businessmen use this fact as an alleged excuse to avoid the mental sweat and courage required by true planning. Instead, they should use it as a pivotal point in their planning.

Time waits for no man; neither does business. Decisions in business must be made as questions arise—even reserving decision till after further study is a decision. The results of a supposed refusal to make a decision can sometimes be more disastrous than a positive "yes" or "no." Planning is not an end unto itself but only a tool to assist in making and then executing decisions. Good planning will advance the time for making these decisions.

One of the most successful companies in the United States—IBM— explains its extensive and costly planning efforts in a very simple way. It says: We are in a highly technical business. Technology is accelerating at an increasing pace. The life span of any decision we make is thereby being increasingly shortened. Our only recourse is to make it sooner and so preserve some of the decreasing payback period. Planning, to us, is a device for advancing the time of decisions and on that basis alone justifies itself.

Any business planning process should in fact be designed to advance rather than delay decisions. It will do this if all thinking and judgments are directed to the future. Thus probable future problems and questions are identified before they fully materialize. No procedure or process can be a substitute for judgment. Therefore, none can assure sound decisions. It should, however, lead to better initial decisions and facilitate modification of them as circumstances require.

The general manager who is faced with the necessity of making a decision concerning any opportunity must, in short, do so immediately on the basis of whatever information and judgments are available. Good planning techniques and practices, *before the time of decision and thereafter,* will provide him with better and more pertinent information and judgments than he would otherwise have.

Minimization of the Risk

The risk that the general manager takes in making an immediate decision on Opportunity No. 1, under the circumstances described, is minimized by the chance to modify it subsequently. But that chance may come too late if it is not assured by continuous planning.

The general manager's risk can also be reduced by the order in which the marketing planner evaluates the different opportunities available to the business. Earlier it was suggested that the easiest way to begin the planning process is to apply it to the product that is currently most important to the business. If this product relates to its "bread and butter" opportunity, as it will in most cases, this is the crucial area for immediate decision on the part of general management. A business, like an individual, reduces its risks by getting its house in order before taking on new responsibilities. After the opportunities vital to immediate survival have been "processed," those essential to future survival—and perhaps some in "greener fields"—can be considered.

The general manager should therefore reject or approve, in original or modified form, the cumulative recommendations concerning Opportunity No. 1 as soon as possible after its review, without waiting for the evaluation of all the other opportunities. He does so on the basis of complete knowledge of No. 1 and incomplete knowledge of the rest. The more opportunities are evaluated and submitted to him, the more his area of incomplete knowledge decreases and he can modify his earlier decisions if necessary.

The planning process also attempts to reduce the risk of decision making initially by calling for the inclusion of certain information and judgments in the functional data concerning Opportunity No. 1; that is, the summary of the cumulative effect which its pursuit, as recommended, will have on

1. Previously planned and scheduled work on other opportunities.
2. Previously evaluated other opportunities still under consideration by the business.
3. Important functional resources.

Prior to more precise identification of these other opportunities and of the direct relation of resources and action programs to their individual pursuit, this summary information may not be too reliable. However, even in the consideration of Opportunity No. 1, the general information provided by each function helps the general manager to get a feel for the possible effect on the currently scheduled activities of the business. Then, as more opportunities are evaluated, this summary information from the functional areas of the company should become more reliable and meaningful for all concerned.

When the general manager decides to pursue Opportunity No. 1, he is saying: "Within the limits of the recommended programs in each functional area, this opportunity has first call on the resources of the business." Later he may have to decide the priority of other opportunities with respect to resource utilization. The functional data on each will give him the benefit of expert thinking and recommendations on this score. For example, the "Manufacturing Data" for Opportunity No. 5 may indicate that with present facilities only half the proposed volume can be produced for the next two years since most of the production resources have been allocated to Nos. 1-4. New facilities can be obtained within two years to handle the required production in full. The general manager must decide how to allocate present facilities; whether to obtain future facilities and, if so, how to allocate them. This decision should not be subject to the convenience or special viewpoint of any one function of the business —whether directly involved in the allocation of resources or not. It should stem from a careful determination of the proper balance between all opportunities.

Strategy is the divining rod for this decision.

The general manager is the ultimate beneficiary of business planning. At the same time he must serve as the pilot, responsible for the strategic thinking which guides the business as a whole in its pursuit of the desired opportunities.

8. The Development of Strategy

In the course of his duties, the general manager is continually choosing between alternatives. Anyone else in the business who makes decisions of any kind is doing the same thing.

The basic difference between the decisions of the general manager and those of the others stems from the authority and responsibility by which they are made. The general manager has responsibility and authority for the business as a whole; therefore, his decisions are intended to guide and control the business as a whole. The other managers have authority and responsibility for a particular area within the business; their decisions are intended to control that area. The decisions of a director of research should concern research activities; those of a manager of marketing, marketing activities; those of a plant manager, plant activities. General management decisions in some manner guide decisions and activities in all areas.

Decisions in one area can establish or change conditions which affect decisions and actions in some one or all of the other areas and to that extent may influence decisions there. For example, a decision by the general manager to produce and sell at least a thousand units of Product X over a five-year period will guide decisions in all functional areas. Marketing must make such decisions as will provide manpower, at the right locations, with the proper knowledge of customer requirements and the skill needed to sell Product X in this quantity. Research and engineering must undertake development that may be required to keep Product X competitive. Manufacturing must assure the most efficient production of X in the specified annual volume and at rates consistent with customer demand. Finance must make funds available to purchase raw materials and labor and to obtain any other resources that are called for.

In this case the general manager may have had many alternatives concerning product and volume. By this decision he has made a choice for the business. By selecting X, a highly engineered product used in electronic circuitry, rather than product Y, a simple consumer product, he has decided which fork in the road is to be taken by the business. Each function will still have alternatives within the area of its activity, although general management's decision will now limit them. Furthermore, its individual choice of alternatives can create conditions which will affect the other functions. For example, marketing's selection of customers will determine the monthly rate of production; one class of customers' demand may be far more seasonal than another's. The line of product development selected by research and engineering can affect alternatives concerning production processes and kinds of customers, and the choice of production facilities can influence product design or financing.

The business obviously cannot operate successfully unless the decisions concerning it as a whole and the decisions concerning all its parts mesh together in a common cause.

Anatomy of a Business Operation

The activities of a business are often labeled a "team" effort. This is a very simple but significant analogy which can be further developed to throw more light on the anatomy of a business operation. If this anatomy is understood, planning and implementation procedures can be tailored to fit it.

Every business operation, large or small, encompasses many skills. Many of these skills have been mentioned under their functional designations: manufacturing, engineering, finance, marketing, and research. The larger the operation in terms of needs served and opportunities pursued, the greater will be the requirements for different kinds and amounts of skills and facilities. And, as these skills and facilities multiply, the problem of their coordination or integration grows geometrically. Awareness of this natural phenomenon of business life has led to recognition of the separate and distinct function in business called general management.

Too often, however, this function is only dimly perceived and, consequently, mismanaged. Many successful engineers, salesmen, financial experts, and manufacturing men, when given the mantle of the general manager, spend most of their time trying to practice their former professions at a higher level. At the very least, they are risking a touch of schizophrenia. Skilled though they may be in their former specialty, their new assignment does not permit them close enough contact with developments in the old field that they can make sound functional decisions. Furthermore, attempts to direct such decisions by making them personally, or by constantly overruling subordinates, dulls the possible contribution of those subordinates and stunts their development. Finally, preoccupation on the part of a general manager with any particular functional area necessarily curtails the time, effort, and thought he can give to the business as a whole.

The general manager, though properly called the "head" of the business, is not supposed to have all the brains. He should, of course, have the authority of *knowledge* as well as the authority of *position* on the organization chart, although an ideal balance is not always attained. This knowledge implies an understanding of the business as a whole and of the means of making it operate as a fully coordinated entity for profitable growth. Definition of the general management function in this way—that is, in terms of its aim—is more meaningful than the now customary description of the kinds of activities which are to be performed in achieving that aim: planning, organizing, integrating (or coordinating), and measuring (or appraising). A general manager must, of course, carry on these activities in some fashion—but so must a lot of other people. In fact, the general manager in a business of any size can do no more than go through the motions without the support of planning, organizing, integrating, and measuring at all organization levels.

Upward, Not Downward

Recognition of the true role of general management, and of the perfectly human limitations of any incumbent of a general management position, forces us to reject as impractical a planning procedure which "starts at the top" of the organization. The late Mark W. Cresap, Jr., while president and chief executive officer of Westinghouse Electric Company, stated the facts forcefully when he said:

The direction of the planning process should be upward, not downward. Planning cannot soundly be centralized. Specific plans should be developed by those responsible for carrying them out within the framework of overall company objectives, policies, and capabilities.[1]

The "top down" approach is suggested by the frequent recommendation that planning begin with a statement of company objectives. This may conjure up a picture of Moses descending from Mount Sinai with the Ten Commandments, but it does not even hint at the source of the knowledge and wisdom required for this more earthly but by no means simple task. True, any thought on the part of top management about company objectives is better than none at all, and any personal effort by a general manager to formalize such objectives may lead to more constructive action along this line by others in the organization. But it is futile for the general manager to try to plan by first closeting himself and coming forth with a list of ready-made goals.

The general manager must, of course, contribute some very essential ingredients to planning for the business as a whole and to planning for every part of it. And that contribution, once made, should guide all subsequent planning. In that sense one *can* say that planning starts with the general manager. A similar statement could be made in recognition of the fact that the attitude of the general manager toward planning usually controls the amount of time and effort that will be devoted to planning. This generalization, however, should not be allowed to misdirect the practice of business planning.

Essentially, the problem of general management's role in planning is one of semantics *and* of concept. Planning doesn't start and stop. Planning continues throughout the life of any business, whether or not it is formalized, efficiently performed, or properly utilized. If the planning process forces the development of all alternatives open to the business and indicates their functional relationships, it will provide the foundation for intelligent decisions by general management.

Basic General Management Guidance

The general manager is both the ultimate beneficiary and the pilot of business planning. Some general management decisions, to be

[1] In "Some Guides to Long-Term Planning," *NACA Bulletin*, January 1963, pp. 601-606.

sure, are more basic to the business as a whole—and more long-term—
than others. When these are made, like the automatic pilot of a plane
they guide progress until the controls are again taken over by the
pilot manually. Falling into this category are:

- General management decisions concerning scope. These operate
  like an automatic pilot to guide marketing and the other
  functional areas in their consideration of needs and opportunities. In the course of identification and evaluation, possible
  modifications of scope may be arrived at, in which case the
  general manager "takes over the controls again" to make a
  decision which resets the automatic pilot.
- General management decisions concerning purpose. General
  management decides the timeless intentions of the business as
  a whole and communicates them through a statement of purpose and interpretive policies which guide all the functional
  areas.
- General management decisions concerning what is here called
  business strategy.

Many strategic decisions are made in the course of running a business, not always by the general manager. There are other important
business decisions which are not strategic. The noun "strategy" and
the adjective "strategic," borrowed from the military, must in fact be
used with some discretion in the business lexicon. Their indiscrimi-
nate use, so in vogue currently, obscures the understanding and insight which they can bring to communication in the business world.

What is strategy in the business sense?

In military usage there are different kinds of strategy. Similarly,
business has a wide variety of strategies, each one distinguished by
the organizational unit or function which develops and applies it. A
look at the nature and relationship of these strategies should reveal
the true business significance of the term and the manner in which
strategy is employed in the planning process.

GENERAL MANAGEMENT STRATEGIES

First, there is strategy for the business as a whole. Since the general
manager has authority and responsibility for the business as a whole,
he must establish such strategy. It is an expression of his judgment; it

is a guide to the entire operation; it outlines the general course of action which is to be followed by the organization *as an entity* in winning its war of survival. As pointed out in Chapter 1, successful survival depends upon the extent to which the business keeps its resources in profitable growth balance with customer needs. What alternative courses of action which are open to the business are most likely to achieve this balance? A decision selecting one or more of these *general* courses of action is strategic. There are three areas for, and means of expressing, general management strategy.

1. Different courses of action are open to a business as a result of the *kinds of customer needs* which it attempts to serve. Obviously, these courses of action are completely different for the company, say, which has chosen to serve the needs of the armed forces for means of guiding certain missiles and the firm which intends to serve the needs of people for sports clothes. Strategic decisions in both cases are made on the basis previously described and are communicated as part of the statement of business scope.

2. Different courses of action are open to a business depending on the *kinds of results* which it seeks to obtain. A company which intends to make a profit through a relatively low volume and high mark-up, like many in electronic and scientific fields, is in a position quite different from that of the company whose intentions are based upon a concept of big volume and low mark-up. Strategic decisions of this sort also are made on the basis described and are communicated in the statement of purpose or policy statements which offer timed interpretations of the various aspects of purpose.

3. Different courses of action are open to a business because of the *kind and amount of resources available* as related to product and service requirements and to competition. These courses of action cannot be identified and evaluated, much less followed, without knowledge of all the available opportunities as described in Chapter 7. Decisions concerning the kinds of opportunities that will be pursued, and the relative emphasis and timing of pursuit, are strategic decisions. They include decisions to pursue only those opportunities which require long production runs suitable for highly automated facilities, or to give priority to those with certain seasonal demands. These decisions should be communicated in the form of a statement of business strategy for the guidance of all functional areas.

The strategy of a business should, in effect, focus everyone's attention on the kinds of opportunities which have the most profitable growth possibilities and direct planning of their pursuit according to their relative possibilities.

- That part of general management strategy which concerns the *kinds of needs* to be served should be long-term.
- That part of general management strategy which concerns the *kinds of results* which must be achieved by the business also should be long-term.
- That part of general management strategy which concerns the *final selection, emphasis, and timing of opportunities* should be both short- and long-term.

FUNCTIONAL STRATEGIES

In addition to general management strategies, there are functional strategies. These depend upon and contribute to the overall business strategy; however, they are distinguished from it and from one another by their strict application to their individual functional areas and activities. After general management decision concerning particular kinds of needs and kinds of results, general courses of action within a functional area which might be suggested by other kinds of needs or results are no longer relevant. The only general courses of action still open to each functional area are those due to the kind and amount of resources available to it. Functional strategies, therefore, concern the kind of specific functional activities that will be performed and the relative emphasis and timing in serving the chosen kinds of needs (scope), in seeking the chosen kinds of results (purpose), and in pursuing the chosen kinds of opportunities (strategy).

What are some specific examples of functional strategies? Marketing decisions like these are typical marketing strategies:

- To utilize independent sales agents rather than the company's own field sales representatives.
- To build a strong independent distributor organization rather than a sales structure within the company.
- To organize and train the sales organization for "specialized" selling rather than general selling.

- To solicit one type of customer rather than all types.
- To market and advertise nationally rather than locally.

By way of further example, these additional decisions represent strategies in the appropriate functional areas:

Research:

- To devote 50 per cent of the available manpower to applied research in a certain technical field rather than in several fields.
- To extend or contract the amount of fundamental research.

Engineering:

- To devote more time to redesign of product than to redesign of manufacturing process so as to obtain desired improvement in cost and quality.
- To obtain outside engineering assistance, as required, rather than build a larger engineering organization.

Manufacturing:

- To lease rather than build facilities.
- To operate on an overtime basis rather than establish a second shift.
- To make rather than buy certain components.

Finance:

- To borrow from banks rather than issue stock whenever funds are required.
- To provide cost and profit information by individual product rather than by manufacturing unit.

STRATEGIC DECISION MAKING IN PRACTICE

To continue the military analogy, strategies—whether for the business as a whole or for one of its functions—concern activities generally "across the board." Their application to specific opportunities is a matter of tactics. A brief explanation of this strategy step in the planning process follows.

Upon completion of the opportunities step, the general manager has before him the cumulative information, judgment, and recommendations of all the functions concerning one particular opportunity. His decision approving or modifying these recommendations will affect, now or later, the ability of the business to pursue other opportunities; therefore, he must be informed of the current and prospective effect on these other opportunities. The marketing and other functional data given him provide some information on this score, and that information becomes more precise and complete as more opportunities are evaluated and presented for general management's approval.

In addition to this information, the general manager must understand or reach a conclusion concerning how important this one opportunity is to the business in comparison with other opportunities. The strategy which he has already developed, or which he must now develop, guides his evaluation. In the course of reviewing this opportunity and gauging its relative importance, he may modify any previously established business strategy. In the latter event, the general manager should inform all concerned of the new business strategy so that they can be guided accordingly and update their own supporting strategies. As suggested, furthermore, each function should be encouraged to give the general manager the benefit of any strategic thinking concerning the business as a whole from its special standpoint. This thinking is invited by the data form outlined in Chapter 7.

On the basis of strategy, an opportunity which offers excellent profit possibilities for the near term may be held in abeyance or set aside because it would interfere with the pursuit of another opportunity with bigger and longer-term profit potential. Or an opportunity with relatively small volume and profit potential may be selected for pursuit because it will build into the business certain capability in a new field. Business strategy is, in short, the basis for selecting among opportunities, for apportioning to each its proper share of the business's resources, and for timing their application.

The practice of business strategy requires knowledge, judgment, and vision on the part of general management. A general manager will find it most difficult, if not impossible, to determine sound business strategy without the information and recommendations provided by the previous planning steps concerned with situation, resources, scope, purpose, and opportunities. Without this background, how can decisions and strategies be of the kind required for a truly customer-oriented business?

Proficiency in strategic decision making leaves little time for meddling in the activities and responsibilities of any of the functional areas of the business—which, as we have seen, is a not uncommon and sometimes disastrous practice.

> A chief executive is on a treadmill to oblivion, unless he takes the time to plan where the company is going. . . . Of course, deciding upon long-range objectives is risk-taking decision making of the highest order. It takes guts to say, "This is where we are going." The whole future of the company is at stake, and it will probably be many years before [he knows whether his] decision is wise. . . . Many chief executives kid themselves into believing they don't have time to think things through, or that it is useless to plan because conditions will surely change. These are rationalizations to hide, even from themselves, their fear of making risk decisions.[2]

The Strategy of Business Growth

> "Which of you by taking thought can add one cubit to his stature?" The obvious answer to this Biblical question is that a man's stature is determined by factors which are beyond his control. In considering the growth and development of a business enterprise it would be easy to slip into the fallacy of assuming that this kind of growth also just happens. Actually the management of any business, by taking thought, can have an important influence on the future size and shape of the business.
>
> Decisions which affect the possibilities for growth may be called *strategic* decisions [italics added]. These major decisions will set the framework within which hundreds of lesser decisions will have to be made. They will affect management's power to act in meeting future problems as they arise. It is true that all long-range decisions are affected by risk since no one can predict the future with certainty. In the same way there are hazards facing the most brilliant military strategist. In facing the prospects, the problems, and the uncertainties of the future, management must give a large measure of its attention to the strategy of business growth.[3]

[2] Robert N. McMurry, *McMurry's Management Clinic*, Simon and Schuster, Inc., New York, 1960, pp. 30-31.
[3] *Cost and Profit Outlook* (a publication of Alderson Associates), April 1951; reprinted in Eugene Kelley and William Lazar, editors, *Managerial Marketing* (revised edition), 1958, p. 295.

There are three stages in the history of a business: establishment, expansion, and stabilization, with the most rapid growth in the middle.[4] These different stages present different strategic considerations and should prompt different strategic decisions by general management and functional management.

Stage 1. The most difficult problems of business strategy face the company which is just starting up or just entering a new field. At such times it is trying to find a place in the market with minimum risk. With resources usually limited to the extent that all possible opportunities cannot be pursued initially, the basic question is, which opportunities should be pursued, when, and how? Maximum sales and profits cannot be expected until later, and then only if a firm position in the market is first established. Such considerations should lead to the selection, for first exploitation, of one kind of opportunity—which might involve a limited product line intended for a limited class of customers. This strategic decision suggests or requires such supporting strategies as advertising and promoting only to this limited class of customer; pricing for selective rather than mass sales; soliciting sales through special rather than mass field agencies; designing a limited rather than a broad line; and buying rather than manufacturing the product (in the event no production capacity is readily available within the company).

Stage 2. When a company has reached the second stage, that of expansion, its aim shifts from a place in the market to a major position which requires outdistancing competition. This calls for maximizing volume and assuming greater risks. More, if not all, kinds of opportunities must be pursued. The overall business strategy requires such new supporting strategies as advertising and promoting widely to all classes of customers; pricing for competitive advantage and mass sales; soliciting sales through all possible field agencies; designing a full line of products, with features equal to or better than those of competitors; building special manufacturing capacity; and financing the expansion through bank loans.

Stage 3. A company in the third stage—that is, stabilization—is more likely to aim at preserving its position while reaping a steady profit. This will probably call for a continuation of the previous business strategy and most of its supporting strategies. However, ad-

[4] The material which follows has been paraphrased from the above-cited publication.

ditional considerations may prompt additional and possibly different supporting strategies. The company's position of leadership in its industry must be considered, as must its image to the public generally and to the government. Different advertising and promotion strategies, even different pricing strategy, may therefore be in order.

It should now be clear that there are no prefabricated or standard sets of either general management or functional strategies which are "subject to call and application" under various circumstances. General management and functional management both should learn from their own experience, and from that of others in similar businesses, that certain kinds of strategies tend to be more successful than others under a given set of general circumstances. But, in the final analysis, all strategies must be custom-made for one particular business in keeping with its situation, resources, scope, and purpose and the judgment and vision of its management.

The Story of Company X

This basic nature of strategies precludes the recitation of one or two simple, concrete, meaningful examples. Only careful, complete study of several businesses over a period of time would suffice. However, to conclude this general discussion with some specifics, the following oversimplified case is offered in summary form.

Our hypothetical Company X is highly successful in the baby food business. Its scope includes only the United States and the service of infants' needs for standard liquid and solid nourishment from the moment of birth until the age of two. The purpose of the company has been stated to cover all the aspects of purpose mentioned in Chapter 6. From time to time it has been interpreted by specific policy statements, one to the effect that growth in volume is desired but not at an accelerated rate which would jeopardize maintenance of the high rate of profit established in the early years of the company's existence.

A few years ago, the company carefully considered the advisability of increasing its scope to cover some of infants' needs for clothing. At that time, general management reaffirmed its previous strategic decision to concentrate on the service of the nourishment needs and in general to ignore the other needs of infants—including those for clothing. The more important considerations leading to this decision were as follows: The company has superior capability to serve these needs with high-quality formulas and specially prepared foods which have had increasing consumer acceptance and are not seriously threatened by any presently perceivable direct or indirect competition. The opportunities connected with the needs promise further growth. The company has increasing knowledge of customer requirements, skill in meeting them, and the means of promoting and selling food products through all channels of distribution as well as direct to the ultimate users; however, these capabilities do not coincide with what would be required to manufacture and sell clothing. Very little of the firm's current assets would in fact be useful in serving the needs for clothing. The company would have to acquire substantial new facilities and know-how, which, though available, would cost a great deal. And, despite the growing needs for clothing, there would be little chance over the long run for a payback similar to that in the food field. The projected profit possibilities are less than the current percentages, and service of the clothing need would in no way buttress the company's present food business or lead directly into some other new area of outstanding opportunities.

For a number of years, the company from time to time considered and rejected the idea of pursuing any food opportunities outside the United States. These more or less casual decisions were primarily based on the proven business strategy of developing a strong market position—at least 25 per cent of the opportunity—in selected local markets before attempting to open up new ones. Initially this strategy was forced by limited production facilities, finances, and manpower—which precluded any attempt to gain national or seminational market coverage immediately. Later, with fewer overall limitations in these respects, the same strategy seemed dictated by the necessity for, and the problems connected with, the construction and manning of additional, market-oriented production facilities across the country without even serious short-term jeopardy to the profit rate.

This business strategy required and received such supporting functional strategies as the following:

1. *Marketing.* Sales promotion and advertising addressed to expectant and new mothers rather than to the public generally or even to all women. Promotions for field sales efforts by

individual selected market area—at least initially. (Actual marketing programs in the geographic areas differed in timing and substance to meet tactical requirements, but all were consistent with these strategies.) First, and continuing, attention to sales through supermarkets, with its implications for packaging as well as product, promotion, and pricing activities. Accelerated package innovations to gain more shelf appeal and safety and convenience in use.

2. *Manufacturing.* Provision for overnight delivery to all selected market areas (in many instances initially through local public warehouses; then through company-owned warehouses; and finally, in many areas, through local production facilities).

3. *Research and engineering.* Continuing major efforts to develop new and improved formulas and processed foods appealing in appearance and use to new mothers and providing increased nutrition for babies. Secondary, though still important, efforts to increase process proficiency.

With the success of the European Common Market, Company X is faced again—but more urgently—with the question of whether it should enlarge its scope to cover Western Europe or any part of it. In preparation for a decision on this point and the strategic decisions which must follow a positive answer, a marketing research project has been conducted. Preliminary investigation showed that adequate information could be developed by an evaluation of infant nourishment needs in the United Kingdom, France, Italy, and West Germany; so the study is limited to these countries. It develops information and judgments as follows:

1. *Concerning magnitudes of needs and opportunities.* The nourishment needs of babies in the four countries combined are, and will continue to be, in excess of those in the United States. They are now, and will continue to be at least through 1970, greatest in West Germany, with France, the United Kingdom, and Italy following in that order. Opportunities for formulas are now relatively small everywhere (owing to the competition from mother's milk), with the greatest promise of growth in West Germany, France, United Kingdom, and Italy (in the order named). Opportunities for processed foods are now substantial in all countries but Italy, with the greatest

demand in the United Kingdom followed by West Germany and France. However, the greatest future growth is expected in West Germany, next in France and the United Kingdom, and finally in Italy.

This kind of information, plus a consideration of expected Common Market developments, may lead to a strategic decision by general management that if scope is enlarged to cover any one of these countries it should cover the others—and, for good measure, the rest of Western Europe. It should raise, but not answer, the question whether any geographic enlargement of scope should at this time cover both needs or only the one served by processed foods.

2. *Concerning product and service requirements and competitive ability to meet them.* According to the study, these requirements differ from those prevalent in the United States and differ from country to country abroad. In no respect, however, do the differences create any problems for Company X from the standpoint of technology. Direct competition in the service of both needs is strongest in the United Kingdom, practically nonexistent in Italy (except by way of imports), and growing stronger in West Germany and France (particularly through joint ventures between local and U.S. businesses). Indirect competition—especially with respect to opportunities for formulas—is greatest in Italy and France.

Baby food businesses are affected by different economic, social, and political factors in each country, and some of these can be expected to persist notwithstanding the influence of the Common Market. For example: Differentials in labor rates (wages are now highest in the United Kingdom and lowest in Italy) will decrease, but probably will never be eliminated altogether. Labor is in extremely short supply in West Germany. The raw materials of food are more readily available and cheapest in France. Packaging materials—a major expense item—are readily available in all countries with minor differences in cost. Food producers in general are favored politically, especially in France, where an obvious long-term effort is being made to establish that country as the primary food source for the Common Market.

Such information, coupled with that on needs and opportunities, may increase the interest of X's general management
and direct its thinking toward either France or West Germany
as the most favorable point of entry.

If the baby food opportunities which have thus far been identified
and evaluated generally are to be measured more precisely from the
particular standpoint of Company X before final decisions are made,
some guidelines are required:

1. Is X interested in serving the two needs in all four countries
   plus the rest of Western Europe? If the answer is "yes," over
   the long term but not necessarily over the short term, a
   strategic general management decision has been made (at least
   tentatively) to enlarge the company's scope accordingly.
2. Is X interested in any of the foreign opportunities if they do
   not contribute to the purpose of the business as stated and
   interpreted domestically? A strategic decision could be made
   to the effect that all the foreign opportunities must satisfy
   purpose as it has been understood and, in addition, must hold
   promise of a specified higher profit to compensate for the
   greater risk.
3. Is X interested in acquiring foreign resources which will permit it to pursue immediately all the opportunities connected
   with both needs in all of Western Europe? General management may decide, as a matter of business strategy, to consider
   obtaining only such foreign resources as may be required to
   pursue only the processed-food opportunities in one of the
   four named countries. This strategy may reflect not only the
   desire to minimize risk but the hope of applying the company's
   successful domestic market-by-market development program.
   It may also reflect the belief that the best way to compete in
   the Common Market of the future is from a very strong
   initial position in one of the leading treaty countries.

These guidelines will probably indicate to Company X's general
management that further evaluation should be focused primarily on
the processed-food opportunities in Western Germany and France.
This evaluation should take the form of business planning statements on these opportunities from the standpoint of similar types of

operations in each country, concentrating on the respective domestic opportunities over the initial short term and on Common Market and Western European opportunities over the long term.

Such statements cannot be prepared without first determining what resources are available in each location, how they can be acquired, what else is needed, and how soon an effective operation can be established. With the situation element provided by the marketing research study, the resource element determined by further special investigation (or assumed within certain limits), and the scope and purpose element provided by X's general management, the suggested business planning process can now be applied to see what can be accomplished through the alternative entry points. When this process has been completed, general management should have a sound basis upon which to make its final decisions concerning Western Europe.

Hard-nosed, practical results are the natural output of this business planning process and the customer-oriented approach of which it is a major part. To this end, objectives and targets must be established to assist management not only in planning but in integrating and measuring business operations. These objectives and targets are, in fact, the primary basic reference points for evaluating the progress of programs and personnel and of their contribution to further planning in the future.

9. Objectives and Targets: Results and Action Programs

LET US CALL THE EXPECTED, OR HOPED-FOR, RESULTS of our business operations, at any particular point in time, *objectives*. Then let us label the action programs to be carried out by the business in gaining those objectives *targets*. At first glance, this may appear to be a play upon semantics, but it is not. Other, perhaps better, terms might be used—as for any of the other special concepts underlying this book. There is, however, no substitute for the intended meaning of the words "objectives" and "targets" and their implications for the successful manager.

OBJECTIVES

"Results are what count" is a phrase often used to excuse rather than to explain. For instance, it is heard when a particular venture turns out satisfactorily in spite of the way it was handled—in which case it is a left-handed form of recognition for the true significance of this phrase to business. However crudely, it does sum up several of the fundamentals we have previously identified and discussed: A business must succeed in order to survive. Success depends upon the results of the business as a whole. These results must reflect the service of particular customer needs. Therefore, whenever a businessman is thinking about—or, better yet, is trying to establish—objectives for his enterprise, he is coming to grips with a very basic business problem.

The so-called and even more often self-styled practical businessman generally has little use for theory. At his peril he ignores the obvious—that sound practice can stem only from sound theory. Yet because, by his own admission, he is interested only in results, he therefore must be interested in any way of getting *better* results.

How can a practical general manager determine what results, or objectives, he can and should achieve? Intuition is a factor in this determination, however it may be defined. So are experience—though it can be either negative or positive—and judgment, which obviously must lean heavily upon knowledge of all pertinent facts. Of these three, surely judgment is the most important, if for no other reason than that it should also reflect whatever intuition and experience the general manager may have had. Certainly one can safely assume that judgment based on some facts will be better than judgment without any, and that judgment with all the facts will be best.

Stripped of all encumbering explanations of technique and extra dividends, the primary aim of the elements of the business planning discussed thus far is to provide the general manager with all the facts so that he can exercise his best judgment in making decisions. Without this background of information, how can what is described by Lawrence A. Appley as the management factor be properly applied? He suggests:

> The management factor is the impact of positive manager action upon the course of events. It is the activation of pre-determined means toward the attainment of pre-established goals.
>
> The management factor is the "something" a manager does to produce different results from those to be expected if events are left to follow their own course. It is what happens when a manager "does something about it." . . .
>
> When competition threatens the survival of a company, destruction is assured if worry is the only defense. The positive action taken to stop or slow down competitive inroads represents the management factor.
>
> The establishing of a long-term objective does not insure its attain-

ment. A forecast is not a statement of what is going to happen. A projection of past results into the future does not portray the future. Something has to be done about it.[1]

But why should it be necessary to establish objectives in terms of timed results? There are three principal reasons for doing so: first, to guide the enterprise in its current and future efforts; second, to permit correct measurement of the progress of those efforts; and third, to establish a firm base for future planning.

Guidance from Objectives

Let us examine further the business planning process which has been discussed in detail through its strategy element. Only the two wrap-up steps remain.

At this point the general manager should have before him for consideration and decision the cumulative recommendations of all the functional areas by individual opportunity: marketing, research, engineering, manufacturing, finance, and—in addition—law, personnel administration, and any other specialties. If he accepts these recommendations without change, he is merely confirming their own suggested marching orders; if his decision modifies their proposal, he is issuing new marching orders. In either event, it is desirable that these orders be clearly expressed and understood—now and in the future—to assure integrated execution. All the areas of specialization must be in step and headed in the same direction.

Expression of these orders formally, in writing, is not the same as casting them in concrete, although some people seem to think so. Orders must change in time just like everything else. This change— and, more importantly, everyone's understanding of it—is facilitated, not handicapped, by the written word. General managers have been known to resist the discipline of writing on the theory that their businesses are too dynamic; they maintain that paperwork cannot keep up with changing circumstances and decisions. When they take this stand, they must recognize that their subordinates have only two alternatives: either to improvise on their own with changing conditions and hope to find, not only the right direction, but the one which is being followed by their associates; or to return to the general

[1] *The Management Evolution,* American Management Association, Inc., 1963.

manager constantly for reassurance or new instructions. The former can lead to chaos and the latter to interminable, wasteful conferences. (Can this be a clue to one of the reasons internal conferences are almost the sole pastime of some managers in our larger companies?)

Dynamic conditions more than any others demand written orders, particularly if any number of people are involved. Without written orders, how can people understand, much less follow, a series of changes in marching orders?

The question is, not whether to formalize, but what to write and how to use it. If there is a clear understanding on these two points, perhaps there will be less reluctance to put decisions in writing. Of course, those who blindly hope to succeed through improvisation and luck, and who fear any precise measurement of their performance, will always resist formalization of their thinking and decision making. And luck and improvisation will always be important ingredients in business success. Written orders and formal planning merely facilitate their full exploitation.

What should be written? As little, not as much, as possible. The essential points should be formalized, not all the details.

Marching orders are most succinctly stated in terms of the specific results to be achieved and the time of achievement. They are most readily understood in these terms. What specifically is to be accomplished and when? That is the payoff question. The answer is an objective—what will be accomplished by the business as a whole and when. Some understanding, but only general direction, is provided by a statement to this effect: "We must make more sales and profit in 1962." But one finds it difficult to misunderstand the same objective stated in more precise terms: "We must sell 1,000 units in 1962. And we must make a profit equal to 8 per cent of sales."

This understanding of what results are expected and when will permit—even require—any further planning and action necessary to insure these, and not some other, results. Of course, the establishment of an objective, whether for the business as a whole or for a particular function, is no guarantee that it will be achieved. If, however, it is properly communicated, it should lead to whatever implementation is possible and can reasonably be expected.

Unfortunately, there is a critical amount of confusion in business circles about objectives; that is, the forecasting—and statement in writing—of the end results to be achieved. Says E. Kirby Warren:[2]

> The fundamental reason for making forecasts is the desire to estimate as accurately as possible the expected outcome of a number of controllable and uncontrollable actions. Despite this . . . many forecasters [feel] that their projections often have to represent what management wants to see, rather than what they are likely to see. . . .

And Mr. Warren points to still another line of reasoning that is responsible for poor forecasting:

> One executive explained it this way: "We can estimate what kinds of changes are likely to occur, but for the most part we are just guessing. Rather than base our plans on guesses, we assume that the future will be largely a continuation of current trends. We know that many of our assumptions will prove incorrect, but so would our guesses. This way we have something to start with that can be modified as we approach the time period involved and greater certainty."

> . . . Thus, even the type of change that is quite certain—change the company is actively working on—is often ignored in preparing forecasts and planning assumptions. The usual explanation is that, although change will result, "it is hard to predict the specific impact of this change."

Whenever an objective is established, it must be determined in view of the understanding, at that time, of all the future circumstances. Lacking clairvoyant foresight, the manager setting the objective must rely on judgment. The planning steps described and their sequence are designed to foster *informed* judgment by general managers and by managers of functional areas. Even so, their judgment will not be infallible. Circumstances will seldom, if ever, develop exactly as anticipated; the change in circumstances may be favorable or unfavorable to the objective. If this change is favorable, every effort should be made to make the most of the possibilities. The volume or timing originally specified should be no deterrent to greater or earlier accomplishment than expected. For example, assume that Company X is introducing a new product late in 1966 directed toward the needs of one group of customers and, on that

2 Warren, E. Kirby, "Where Long-Range Planning Goes Wrong," *Management Review*, May 1962, pp. 4-15.

basis, anticipates and establishes a volume objective of 1,000 units for 1967. If a new group of customers is found early in 1967 whose needs can be served by the same product in combination with another, certainly every effort should be expended to capitalize on this additional volume. If, on the other hand, the change in circumstance is unfavorable to the objective, every effort should be made to minimize the effect on volume or timing of anticipated results. Suppose that Company X did not discover the new potential and instead found that the first group of customers needed the product but were unable to afford it temporarily because of sudden, adverse economic conditions in their industry. In either event, the establishment of the objective and the planning and implementation in support of it assure better results than would have been possible without any objective.

These comments may seem to suggest that objectives should be modified constantly. Quite the contrary! They should be modified only with major changes in circumstances. Constant amendment, in response to every change in the wind, not only creates unnecessary paperwork but confuses the entire organization. Certainly objectives should not be amended automatically whenever it appears that they will be either exceeded or not fully achieved. If they still give the right kind of direction and guidance, it is neither necessary nor desirable to change them. Objectives are not part of a game requiring either performance to match them or modification to match performance.

As a matter of routine, it may be advisable to review and update objectives once a year. For some kinds of businesses and for some kinds of opportunities, more frequent review and modification may be desirable. This is a matter of judgment in each case. In the simple example of Company X, it would seem advisable to modify the volume objective immediately in the first instance though not in the second. By evaluating the additional volume to be obtained from the new group of customers and by increasing the volume objective accordingly, management will be providing desirable guidance for the exploitation of this new opportunity. But, by leaving the volume objective unchanged in the event of adverse economic conditions, management will at least be providing sufficient guidance to make the best of the situation.

Objectives as Measurement Reference Points

The second use of objectives, to permit correct measurement of progress, is in many respects only an extension of the first.

Management must periodically measure the performance of all programs and activities (1) to be sure their progress is satisfactory, (2) to know when and how to modify or supplement them, and (3) to know how to reward those who are carrying them out. In all logic and fairness, the basic reference points for measurement should be the same in all three respects. Obviously, intelligent management would not on the one hand find that a certain program is progressing very satisfactorily and at the same time reward the man in charge as if he were performing below standard or think of modifying the program itself.

What, then, should be the common reference points? The expected results or objectives, of course! Their use is the first fundamental requirement for sound measurement in business. If we don't have this kind of yardstick, we grasp at anything else that may be available or don't even pretend to measure performance.

Measurement is required at all levels and in all units of the organization and for all activities, whether they are continuing or special programs. In each instance, particular knowledge and techniques may be required, and special circumstances may have to be considered. For example, measuring the progress of a research project or the contribution of an individual research man is very different from measuring the progress of a program to build a new factory. In both, however, and all other instances, the principle applies that measurement should have as its basis expected results—objectives. This is the most important, if not the only, point common to all measurement throughout a business.

If all the objectives established for activities of all the organizational levels and units are coordinated or integrated in a common cause, the differences in techniques and circumstances at each point of measurement will be positive factors in advancing that common cause. If the objectives are not integrated, these differences will represent divergent forces which will scatter the activities of the enterprise in all directions. Therefore, the second fundamental requirement for sound measurement is a framework of integrated objectives throughout the entire organization.

In broad outline, what is involved in building this framework? First, the aim of this structure must be established. As previously implied, it is to provide the foundation for a system of directing and evaluating all activities throughout the business on an integrated or coordinated basis. Second, the focus for integration must be understood. This focus, clearly, is the service of particular customer needs. Since such service involves two time perspectives, the present and the future, the focus must be adjusted to both. Third, the activities of the business must be recognized, and objectives for them established, from the standpoint of this focus. This means that every activity must be recognized for what it can and must contribute, now and in the future, to the service of particular customer needs, rather than for its area of specialization. Which is just another way of saying a business must be truly customer-oriented.

This approach should lead us to set objectives for all activities from two perspectives: first, the extent to which they are directed toward the application of resources to opportunities; second, the extent to which they are directed toward the maintenance and development of resources. These perspectives cut across areas of specialization. With them, the general manager should have a real understanding of the business as a whole and of its current and future prospects for success. Within each area of specialization, moreover, the functional manager—as well as the general manager—gains an understanding and appreciation of the role that function is expected to play as part of the business team.

Objectives for the business as a whole, so established, not only guide the enterprise generally but provide a specific framework for integrating any and all supporting functional objectives and action programs throughout the business. They not only fix the basic reference points for all measurements of the enterprise but provide a specific framework for integrating any and all supplementary measurements throughout the business.

The planning process contemplates and provides means for establishing these kinds of objectives. To the extent it does so, not only is this process important to the general manager for the aid it gives him in his *planning* responsibilities, but it also helps him in carrying out his *integrating* and *measuring* responsibilities.

Objectives and the Application of Resources

If the previously described steps in planning are followed, at some point in time all recognizable opportunities for the business will have been identified and evaluated from the standpoint of their volume and profit possibilities. All functions will have recommended whether each opportunity should be pursued, how, and with what results for the business. On this basis, general management—with the aid of strategy—will have selected those opportunities which are to be pursued and determined their relative emphasis and timing.

Marching orders for each opportunity will then have been issued. These orders, in the form of objectives, should tell everyone *generally* to what extent, and when, currently available and anticipated resources are to be applied to individual opportunities; but, at the same time, they should tell everyone *specifically* what expected results are to be achieved. Hence the business organization requires more detailed directions concerning the timed application of particular resources. These directions can be communicated by specifying volume objectives, market position objectives, and profit objectives for each opportunity *and the nature of the principal action programs to support these objectives.*

TARGETS

For ready reference, these principal action programs have been called *targets.* They indicate the *how* and *when* for the objectives' *what* and *when. Targets are the planned, timed steps to be taken by the business on the road to each opportunity.* They are the planned daily mileages, and the overnight stops, on the way to the ultimate destination or objectives.

Volume, market position, and profit objectives should have been established only after careful consideration of the principal action programs which must be taken to achieve them. Outlining these action programs as targets confirms for all concerned the need to implement them in the manner and time contemplated.

While objectives succinctly state the marching orders, targets amplify and explain them. Targets go hand in hand with objectives.

Together the two indicate what results are expected and when; they show how the business will try to achieve these results.

The spelling out of major action programs and their timing does not preclude their later modification to coincide with developing circumstances. Instead, it facilitates evaluation by general management and everyone concerned of the advisability of any future change that may be proposed. For example, the volume, market position, and profit objectives of Opportunity No. 1 in 1966 may depend upon full development and successful pilot production in 1965 of Product X. Possibilities for further improvement of Product X, discovered in mid-1965, should not be automatically rejected because they will delay the introduction of the product until mid-1966. However, a decision to incorporate their improvement in the product should not be made without careful consideration of the exact effect it will have on the achievement of the objectives for 1966 *and later years.*

The designation of targets not only facilitates more careful evaluation of possible changes in major programs necessitated by actual circumstances; it also prompts early, rather than late, evaluation. The effect of change on programs is not always as obvious as that cited in our example. If an action program which concerns, say, manpower is not directly related to volume, market position, and profit objectives, little recognition is likely to be given to the harmful effect which any change in it may have on certain opportunities. For example, an across-the-board reduction of the research budget in times of trouble usually means a reduction in manpower. But, if that manpower and its know-how have been directly related to specific opportunities available to the business, as well as to its broad areas of interest, the necessary reduction can be made in a way which will have the least harmful consequences.

Targets, along with objectives, also serve as a continuing device for integrating planning and action in the different functional areas of the business. To return to the planned introduction of Product X, designating the nature and timing of the development work aids manufacturing in precise planning and preparation for pilot production. It also permits other functions to set up their respective programs in the proper sequence. Any planned delay, and the consequent change in one program, should take into account and trigger specific changes in others. Management may, in fact, capitalize on such changes, rather than merely minimize their harmful effects, if they are anticipated and made sufficiently early in the game.

Organized Consideration and Communication

This rationale for targets not only justifies the trouble involved in their formal designation but also suggests means of expressing and communicating them.

Important perspective for a full understanding of volume, market position, and profit objectives is provided by taking care always to relate these objectives expressly to the magnitude of *both* the need and the opportunity with which they are connected. This relationship can be clearly shown by a written statement following the format used in evaluating each opportunity.

	Historic Record				Current Year	Future for Planning Period			
	1950	1955	1960	1964	1965	1966	1967	1968	1969
Need (units or $)	100	200	300	350	400	500	600	700	800
Opportunity (units or $)	100	200	200	250	300	300	400	500	600
Volume objective (units or $)	50	100	100	100	100	150	200	250	300
Market position objective:									
% to need	50	50	33	28	25	30	33	36	31
% to opportunity	50	50	50	40	33	50	50	50	50

These objectives, it should be recalled, were developed after the identification and cumulative consideration of the critical conclusions and assumptions concerning needs, customers, and competition and the special action programs of each function. They therefore reflect a commitment on the part of all the functions, and of general management, to carry out the special action programs as agreed on. They also represent a judgment that the results specified can be achieved if these programs are executed as planned under the projected circumstances.

It is therefore recommended that, accompanying the statement of objectives, there appear a written statement of the three kinds of critical conclusions and assumptions, each followed by a summary (in the briefest form possible) of any special programs to be undertaken by individual functions. These summaries should indicate what each program is designed to accomplish in relation to the conclusion or assumption, when it is to be accomplished, and what course of action is to be followed. Every effort should be made to avoid detailing functional activities; ample target information should be readily available in the functional data described in Chapter 8, pages 133-134, and in any record of general management thinking and decision during its review of the cumulative recommendations concerning the opportunity. Many programs will, of course, be directed toward several conclusions—particularly different conclusions concerning needs, customers, or competition. Unnecessary and undesirable repetition can be avoided by simple cross-reference.

There are several benefits to be derived from organizing and expressing targets in this manner. The process reveals to what extent action is planned concerning each critical point, which functions are responsible for what and when, and how one function's action is interrelated with action in another function on specific matters. Thus it provides not only a basis for finally checking to insure that enough programs have been planned (and the right kind) but also a mechanism for integrating functional planning and execution. If future developments indicate that the original conclusion or assumption was incorrect, all the dependent programs can be easily identified and modified. In addition, this method of spelling out targets permits some measurement of total progress toward objectives, as well as integration of short-term adjustments in scheduled action.

OBJECTIVES PLUS TARGETS

The establishment of objectives and targets establishes a common basic reference point against which all functions can determine whether, in their individual statements of planning, they have provided the necessary supporting programs for each and every opportunity.

Maintenance and Development of Resources

A business which has identified all its opportunities and has established volume, market position, and profit objectives for each, with supporting targets, is well along the road of sound business planning. However, one very important aspect of planning is still missing: the maintenance and development of resources *as such*.

The targets supporting the volume, market position, and profit objectives will of course direct how certain resources are to be used and, in some cases, what resources are to be developed and when. However, the perspective on resources that is so provided is "piecemeal" rather than total. Every prudent car owner will occasionally check the air in his tires and the water in his battery and will regularly fill his gas tank before each long trip; he would never think of omitting periodic, overall check-ups and preventive maintenance. In the same way every business requires its own 1,000- and 5,000-mile check-up on resources.

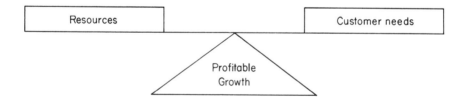

The crux of business success, as Chapter 2 pointed out, is the profitable growth balance between customer needs and resources. In order to achieve and maintain this balance, a business must properly apportion its resources to specific needs and individual opportunities, but the resources in total must "weigh the right amount." This right amount for the future can be determined only if specific and careful attention is directed to resources, as such is the key to any sound cost control.

This analysis of resources should be made from the standpoint of the needs of the company as distinguished from customer needs. If the objectives and targets for all opportunities do not require a certain production facility, it is not needed by the business and will retard profitable growth. On the other hand, if the objectives and targets for all opportunities require additional production facilities, failure to obtain them will stunt the growth of the business.

The company's needs for manpower can be similarly measured, as well as the kinds of skill and know-how which will be required. These types of resources can be related to objectives and targets rather easily, with respect to both quantity and quality. With intangibles such as reputation with customers or the public, it is a little more difficult.

On the basis of this analysis, objectives should be established for each important resource. It may not be possible, in all cases, to specify expected results in as precise terms as, say, quantity. However, some degree of exactness as to their nature, as well as their timing, should be feasible. In any event, the objectives should also be supported by timed action programs or targets.

The general manager has responsibility and authority for the maintenance and development of all the business resources. In effect, he assigns some of these to each functional area and holds the functional manager responsible for their maintenance and development. The manager then should recommend objectives and targets for the resources entrusted to him. This he can do in the course of preparing and submitting his statement of functional planning for general management review and approval.

Business resources which are not so assigned must be covered by objectives and targets established by the general manager. Furthermore, he must establish objectives and targets for the sum total of all the company's resources: those which have been assigned to individual areas of specialization and those which have not. He must understand their relationships to one another and their capabilities in combination. For example, the general manager must be satisfied that the research function's program for maintenance and development of resources is adequate not only from the standpoint of research but from that of the business as a whole.

To be sure, research's planning should be expressed in terms of the business as a whole; however, the general manager has responsibility and final authority in this matter.

The manager is aided in reaching a decision by projecting research's planning against scope and purpose. By so doing he may find that research is planning all the manpower and know-how required for the proper pursuit of all presently known and scheduled opportunities, but he may also find that no research effort is planned in a field which can affect some needs within the scope of the business. Or he may find that the manpower development program in research is lagging behind similar programs in other areas of specialization. In such instances, he will probably order changes only in the objectives and targets established by research for its maintenance and development of resources. However, if the general manager should find that research was making progress and planning still further efforts in a field which could develop technical capabilities to serve new needs, some of them beyond the present scope of the business, modifications might be required in the planning of other functional areas.

Reference Points for Personal Reward

The use of objectives and targets in evaluating and rewarding individual performance has been mentioned briefly. This whole subject of compensation and incentives is too complex and important to be treated summarily; however, some basic guidelines emerge from the planning process and from the customer-oriented approach to business operations of which it is a principal part. These guidelines, with related thoughts, are noted here for the light they throw on this book's theme.

1. *The primary reference point for personal incentive and compensation should be expected, timed results or objectives.* Nothing is more important to an individual in business—or in any other activity—than the results of his performance. Nothing about any individual within a business enterprise should be more important to management.
2. *The precise formulation of objectives gives an individual and his superiors a succinct understanding of the general direction of his activity and the expected end results.* The precise formulation of supporting targets further clarifies and details this mutual understanding by spelling out the methods to be employed and the progressive timed steps to be taken.

    Such an understanding of the basis of personal evaluation

and compensation is essential for fairness and acceptance by all concerned. It also permits continuing self-measurement by the individual which should lead to earlier correction and improvements.

3. *The derivation of an individual's objectives and their supporting targets from a framework of integrated objectives for the organization as a whole provides more meaning and therefore incentive to the individual.* It also develops a favorable climate for understanding and cooperation among individuals as they work toward a common cause. Almost everyone's performance in a business can affect and is affected by the performance of others. And as this interrelationship becomes known more clearly, it can be taken into account as a part of any performance appraisal.

4. *The validity of objectives as primary personal measurement reference points is not destroyed by their changeability or lack of infallibility.* When it is appropriate to change them for business guidance, it is also appropriate to consider them changed for use in measurement of individual performance. Circumstances may develop in a completely unexpected way. It is quite possible that superior performance will sometimes be reflected by less-than-specified results, and vice versa. Moreover, objectives often are distorted by those who establish them; some people estimate conservatively while others, either unconsciously or intentionally, are more optimistic.

5. *The best objectives, from the standpoint of the business and each individual within it, are those which are neither optimistic nor conservative but are realistic and yet challenging.* In evaluating individual performance, moreover, it is important to measure not only actual results against such objectives but also participation in establishing objectives which are truly realistic and challenging.

Whether or not an objective can be so categorized depends upon what results are possible under all the circumstances. Recognition of this principle forces us to conclude that an objective established solely on the basis of past performance cannot be realistic and challenging. Future circumstances are bound to be different in some respects; they, rather than past circumstances, should be controlling.

This means, for example, that a volume objective for a specific opportunity which is determined solely by projecting the trend of past yearly increases or decreases in sales is suspect on its face. It also means that the objective of increasing research or sales manpower by X per cent over the *next* five years, simply because that has been the percentage of increase during the *past* five years, is questionable. Past experience is helpful in establishing realistic and challenging objectives only if that experience is projected into soundly forecast future circumstances.

Objectives are *realistic* when the results specified are possible in amount and in time. A volume objective will not be realistic if it exceeds the customer need from which it sprang (this is one of the reasons for determining the magnitude of the need). In the same way, an objective which calls for developing a new product from scratch within a two-year period, when all experience in the field indicates that four to five years will be required, is probably not realistic.

Objectives are *challenging* if the results are possible but are attainable only if maximum effort is expended to achieve them. A volume objective which reflects a 40 per cent share of the total opportunity is generally more challenging than one reflecting a 30 per cent share, particularly if the business has historically enjoyed only 25 per cent (this is one of the reasons for determining the magnitude of the opportunity and market position). And an objective requiring the development of a new product within four years will be more challenging than one specifying a five-year period.

Objectives which are established without a basis of informed judgment are realistic and challenging only through happenstance. It is difficult enough, even so, to arrive at just the right amount of challenge. To quote E. Kirby Warren on this point:

> In many cases, programs laid out for years two to five of a five-year plan fail to reflect more than a degree of qualified effort in this area. Because of inadequate forecasting, the best possible picture of the expected future state has not been drawn. Therefore, to begin with, objectives are necessarily arbitrary, since they reflect neither an accurate projection of the external environment nor an accurate projection of internal change. . . .
>
> If a best effort is made and falls short of perfection, those involved,

knowing that their best efforts are expected, will . . . perhaps be stimulated; but where the best is not demanded and less meaningful efforts are accepted, the first people to realize that "not much is expected of our plans" are those working on them.[3]

Objectives which are unrealistic, which either lack challenge or impose too much of it, misdirect the business—with consequent waste of resources and loss of opportunity. Nor do they provide fair reference points for the measurement of individual performance. No one whose performance is evaluated on such a basis will develop to his full potential, even if temporarily he be rewarded more than he deserves.

In the absence of objectives established on a basis of informed judgment directed toward the profitable growth of the business as a whole, we should not be surprised to find such conditions as these— which are so prevalent they may even constitute the rule rather than the exception throughout American business:

- Sales quotas for units and individual salesmen which are so low that some people virtually retire near the end of the quota period, or which have been known to inspire manipulation of orders to the advantage of individuals and the disadvantage of the business.
- Sales quotas which are too high and therefore affect compensation unfairly and dull sales efforts.
- Sales and marketing compensation geared only to short-term volume, even at the expense of the long term.
- Manufacturing bonuses based on improved production efficiencies which have little bearing and, in some cases, an adverse effect upon the service of particular customer needs in a manner equal to—or better than—competition.
- Engineering and research compensation governed more by size of budget and number of personnel than the amount and timing of specific contributions to the profitable growth of the business.
- General management compensation dependent upon the realization of certain volume and profit goals established primarily by the dead hand of the past and manipulated by personal, opportunistic, and short-term considerations.

[3] *Op. cit.*, pp. 10-11.

Firm Base for Future Planning

It may be appropriate here to repeat the trite yet profound slogan, "Plan your work, and work your plan." The most carefully drawn statement of planning is of little value if it is simply filed away in the bottom drawer for possible use later on as an excuse.

Yet the effort involved in preparing even that statement has not been entirely wasted. Management has been known to say that planning would be worthwhile even if the statement were destroyed. That is true because the statement is a means rather than an end unto itself. The only way to get real mileage from a statement of planning is to put it to immediate and continuous use. But it is the servant, not the master.

A statement of planning can be one of the most useful management tools for guiding the current and future efforts of the business if it is properly conceived, clearly and concisely stated, and kept current. It can be one of the most useful management tools for measuring the progress of programs and personnel, and for further planning in the future, if these same conditions are satisfied.

When it is suggested that planning should be a continuous activity, which is properly depicted in the form of a circle, this is not to recommend that it be a repetitive exercise, with the same or even different people going over the same ground time and time again. Rather, it is recommended that systems and procedures be adopted which will avoid the confusion and the waste of time and effort which result from such unorganized efforts. The correct approach to business planning will in some manner provide for finalizing the output of everyone's work, at any point in time, so that it can be used as a stepping stone for further planning. And that stepping stone will not be firm if it does not include, among other things, formalized objectives and targets. The "other things" are, of course, the records of findings, conclusions, recommendations, and decisions described in the chapters on opportunities and strategy. The firm base so provided permits the continuation or renewal of planning with minimum effort and with maximum understanding of past experience.

Not only is this base firm; but, as indicated, it reflects integrated planning and action. It therefore leads to integrated planning, measurement, and action in the future.

How should planning be put in writing? What should be included and how? General management of course establishes the basic format. Then, first of all among the functional statements, comes that of marketing planning. Within the frame of reference thus provided, format and content for the other areas of specialization can be determined and for the statement of general management's own planning.

10. Formats for Planning Statements

THIS SUGGESTED PLANNING PROCESS—LIKE ANY other—requires, as we have seen, written records of our thinking. The tedious but worthwhile distillation which comes only from setting our thoughts down in writing cannot be avoided. It is a planning "must." However, like all good things, it can be overdone if it is not controlled. There are two major control points, one at the input and the other at the output stage.

The first control is exercised through the kind of planning process adopted. That described in this book is a disciplined approach designed to direct thought and effort to *only those matters which are essential*—despite the fact that the first attempt to apply it fully is likely to generate unnecessarily voluminous information. Experience indicates that we can become so enamored with data gathering that we make unconscious excursions into areas which appear to be interesting but later prove relatively unimportant. These excursions are not without benefit to the planner because he thereby sharpens his discretion for the future; however, under some circumstances they can be expensive to the business and dampening to the enthusiasm. For example, one enthusiastic novice spent months developing and writing up great quantities of detail concerning customers and competition generally but failed to identify specific needs and opportunities. Without this sharp focus, he was too tired to make his critical conclusions and assumptions and to recommend, on that basis, specific action programs and results.

The second control is by way of regulating what is done with the written record generated by the process. The output of a gasoline refinery is not profitably utilized until the different octanes are separated and diverted to their intended end uses. So it is with the output of the business planning process. Some parts of the record are important to certain functions and the holders of certain positions within those functions. Other functions and the holders of other positions are more interested in quite different parts—say, the information summaries as opposed to the complete details. The planning process should generate all that is necessary, but the total body of information must be separated and presented in different ways suited to the different end uses anticipated. Otherwise, people will be overwhelmed with paper.

Townsend Hoopes, of Cresap, McCormick and Paget, management consultants, suggests that "all sound business planning begins with a planning format" which must be formulated by top management. He says:

> Devising the planning format, which involves selecting the elements to be contained in the plan and determining their arrangement and relative emphasis, is a major undertaking. A basic format will be subject to refinement over the years, but it represents the stable framework within which the variable planning estimates are presented from year to year. In a functionally organized company, the format will normally be divided along functional lines, with separate sections for research, manufacturing, marketing, and other important activities. There will also be a consolidated summary plan. In a divisionalized company, the format will usually provide a separate plan for each division and a consolidated summary.*

In Chapter 7 the unique interests of the different functions were recognized. It was suggested there that each function should prepare its own statement of planning. This statement would include a record of such thinking employed in the function's planning as might be germane to its operations. It would also include the sup-

---

* "The Corporate Planner" (New Edition), *Business Horizons*, Vol. 5, No. 4, Winter 1962.

porting details which were developed and summarized in the course of that planning, or which might be required to assure the function's proper contribution to the objectives established for the business.

Statement of Marketing Planning

By way of fuller explanation and illustration, a suggested format for a "Statement of Marketing Planning" is outlined here.

SECTION I: BUSINESS OBJECTIVES/TARGETS

A. *Total Objectives.* Setting forth the historical record and the expected yearly results over the planning period for volume, market position, and profit for the *total of all opportunities* to be pursued by the business.

B. *Objectives/Targets by Individual Opportunities.* Setting forth the historical record and the yearly projections over the planning period for each need and for each opportunity; also, the expected yearly results in volume, market position, and profit—all in table form as follows:

	Historic Record 1950 1955 1960 1964	*Current Year* 1965	*Future for Planning Period* 1966 1967 1968 1969
Need (units or $)			
Opportunity (units or $)			
Volume objective (units or $)			
Market position objective: % to need % to opportunity			

This same information can also be shown most effectively on a semi-log chart. To it should be added the statements of critical conclusions and assumptions concerning needs, customers, and competition, followed by a *summary statement of the major action programs of the business* over the planning period which are directed to each conclusion. Each and every opportunity to be pursued should be so covered.

Wherever programs call for marketing action, marketing targets must be spelled out in such complete detail as is necessary to assure full understanding and execution by the marketing personnel involved. Since this detail is likely to be voluminous and of little interest to others, it should be included as the last section of the statement.

SECTION II: MARKETING STRATEGY. As described in Chapter 8.

SECTION III: OPPORTUNITIES. Describing *summarily* the kind of opportunities which are to be pursued and which are covered specifically in Section I. It should also describe all other opportunities which have been identified and the decisions concerning them— for example, to postpone further considerations of Opportunity *X* but to continue studying Opportunity *Y*.

SECTION IV: PURPOSE OF MARKETING

A. Marketing's Recognition of, and Allegiance to, the Purpose of the Business. Can be expressed by a statement to the effect that "within scope and the developing situation, marketing will so utilize resources as to make optimum contributions to the following purpose" (to be accompanied by the appropriate quotation from the company's statement of policy).

B. Objectives/Targets Concerning Maintenance and Development of Resources in Marketing. As described in Chapter 9. Will include, for example, objectives and timed action programs for additional manpower, for the training of salesmen, for job rotation, and for advertising to promote the corporate image. In total, these objectives and targets are related to all opportunities; they provide the foundation upon which marketing makes its unique contribution to the satisfaction of the business's purpose.

SECTION V: SCOPE OF MARKETING. Established by the scope of the business. If this is not restated here, reference should be made to it or a copy attached because it determines certain dimensions of marketing's area of operation. The remaining dimensions are determined by the definition of *marketing's role within the business*, which is best stated and understood by all concerned in terms of aims or expected results. See Chapters 7 and 12.

SECTION VI: SITUATION OF THE BUSINESS. Should contain all marketing's information and judgments concerning needs, customers, and competition as described in Chapter 4. Should be organized by individual needs and opportunities.

SECTION VII: RESOURCES OF THE BUSINESS. Containing all marketing's information and judgments concerning resources, as described in Chapter 5. Should be organized by individual needs and opportunities.

SECTION VIII: OBJECTIVES/TARGETS OF MARKETING. All action programs in such detail as is necessary to permit their direction and measurement. Should be organized by individual needs and specific opportunities.

It is recommended that the "Statement of Marketing Planning" be presented almost in reverse order of the sequence by which the information was developed. This reversal focuses everyone's immediate attention on the payoff area—the expected and planned results. It also is a device for conveying to the reader the significance to the business of all the marketing information and judgments set forth. It does not, however, mean that the sequence of planning in the future will be any different from that explained in Chapters 3 through 9.

Statement of Planning—Other Functions

The format for the statements of research, engineering, manufacturing, and finance planning should differ in some respects from that of marketing.

SECTION I: BUSINESS OBJECTIVES/TARGETS. Will be the same as for marketing except that special emphasis should be given to summaries of action programs planned by the particular function.

SECTION II: STRATEGY OF FUNCTION. Self-explanatory.

SECTION III: A restatement of marketing's section on this subject.

SECTION IV: PURPOSE OF FUNCTION. Will parallel marketing's section but will be written from the standpoint of the particular function.

SECTION V: SCOPE OF FUNCTION. Will parallel marketing's section but will define the specific role of the particular function within the business.

SECTION VI: OBJECTIVES/TARGETS BY FUNCTIONAL ACTIVITY. Will parallel marketing's section but will spell out in detail the functional action programs which are required by Section I. Should be organized by individual needs and specific opportunities.

Sections VI and VII in the "Statement of Marketing Planning" will have no equivalents in these other functional statements. For detailed information on *situation* and *resources*, each function will rely upon copies of marketing's statement. In any case each will have the essential information in the critical conclusions and assumptions concerning needs, customers, and competition included in Section I of its own statement.

This functional format is dictated by the intended use of the statement to guide, measure, and further plan all the function's activities in the future. These activities will include execution of the marching orders given by general management and the development, through planning, of new information, judgments, and recommendations for general management consideration and decision. The statement therefore should provide meaningful direction (integrated with the directions to all other functions), a basis for measuring the progress of functional programs and personnel (integrated with similar measurements throughout the business), and a record of information necessary for continued planning which can be easily updated as required and which can be integrated with the planning being done by the other areas of specialization.

Statement of Business Planning

Similarly, the format for the statement of planning for the business as a whole is dictated by its proper use. It is a tool, a most valuable one, to aid the general manager in fulfilling his role in the business. Accordingly, its format should be as follows:

SECTION I: OBJECTIVES/TARGETS.

A. *Total Objectives.* Like all the functional statements, should set forth the historical record and the expected yearly results over the planning period for volume, market position, and profit for the total of all opportunities to be pursued by the business.

B. *Objectives/Targets by Meaningful Groups or Classes of Opportunities.* As previously noted, the general manager cannot, on a continuing basis, concern himself with details in any function of the business. Neither can he be concerned, on a continuing basis, with each and every opportunity. He should know which opportunities are most important to the future profitable growth of the business and concentrate on them singly, considering the others as one or more groups or classes of opportunities.

Therefore, this section should state which particular opportunities are most significant to the business and why. For each such opportunity, the historical record and the yearly projections over the planning period should be shown in the same manner as in Section I of the "Statement of Marketing Planning"; also, the expected yearly results in volume, market position, and profit. The importance of the opportunity may be highlighted by adding to the table of information the percentage of total business sales and profit which it represents. These projections should be followed by summaries of the critical conclusions and assumptions concerning needs, customers, and competition and the major action programs directed to each. If and when the general manager is interested in more details concerning an opportunity, or the details of the action programs planned by any particular function, he should refer to the appropriate statement of planning.

Similar or related opportunities of less significance can be consolidated and then treated in the same manner.

SECTION II: STRATEGY. As described in Chapter 8.

SECTION III: OPPORTUNITIES. A restatement of marketing's section on this subject.

SECTION IV: PURPOSE. As described in Chapter 6. Also, there should be a complete statement of objectives and targets concerning the maintenance and development of resources for the business as a whole (see Chapter 9).

SECTION V: SCOPE. As described in Chapter 6.

There will be no section on situation and resources. The general manager will rely on the pertinent information contained in the "Statement of Marketing Planning."

The "Statement of Business Planning" in this form and content, supported by the statements of all the various areas of specialization, should provide the general manager with the information, judgment, and past decisions which he must continually have before him in order to guide, measure, and integrate the progress of programs and personnel in all areas of the business against planned results, and in order to initiate or review new information, judgments, or recommendations directed toward further planning for the future profitable growth of the business in keeping with actual rather than merely anticipated developments.

This is not to suggest, even by implication, that the general manager should not review all the functions' statements of planning. He should look them over at least once a year, and at that time approve or modify them. In the meantime, except in cases of special need, he will not be preoccupied with their details but will focus on the overall "big picture."

Just as the systematic measurement of results is an essential part of the management job, so the effectiveness of any particular tool or technique must be determined from time to time. Not only must the planning process be carefully studied before its introduction, but it must be periodically reviewed after installation to see whether, in practice, it is meeting the company's needs and whether improvements may not be possible.

11. Criteria for Evaluating The Planning Process

THE PLANNING PROCESS DEVELOPED IN THESE PAGES can be used in any business, big or small. It does not matter whether a product is involved, a service, or both. The process as described can be used in a centralized or a decentralized organization; in a retail, wholesale, or manufacturing operation. The exact manner of installation and application will differ, of course, with the type of enterprise.

However, this or any other basic process should be fully understood and carefully evaluated *before* it is applied. It should also be re-evaluated from time to time, *after* it has been installed, as part of an organized effort to improve and streamline the process itself and any related procedures.

The previous chapters will have provided the necessary understanding of the business planning process. The following criteria and comments may be useful in evaluating it.

1. Does the process "start" at the right place? Customer Land is the payoff area, the Land of Opportunity for the business. If management does not know who its customers are, what needs they have, who else is trying to serve them, and under what economic, social, and political conditions, how can the business live—much less grow—

in that land? In short, a business must first of all understand its situation.

2. Does the process "end" at the right place? The amount and timing of the payoff are determined by the customers' acceptance, individually and collectively, of the service offered by the business. It would seem, therefore, that the right place to "end" is with the particular timed action which the business will take to serve individual customers (the targets it will aim at). Thus the process outlined in this book "begins" with the general and "ends" with the specifics—both in Customer Land.

3. Does the process follow a straight line between those two points? The interim steps between situation and targets—that is, the elements of resources, scope, purpose, opportunities, strategy, and objectives—must be in proper sequence. Each then (*a*) picks up where the preceding steps leave off, (*b*) extends the substance of all previous steps toward the final point of action, and (*c*) depends upon the subsequent step for fulfillment in application.

4. Does the process recognize the continuous nature of planning? As seen, planning can be depicted as a circle as well as a straight line. Changes in any one element trigger reconsideration of all others. Changes in circumstances, fact, judgments, or decisions ideally are anticipated and easily accommodated at any point in the process.

5. Does the process discard the irrelevant and focus attention on only the relevant information, judgments, and decisions? As described here, it provides this discipline because—

    a. Each step or element represents a separate type of relevancy from a particular, important standpoint of the business. Each step provides its particular perspective on what the business could and should do for profitable growth.

    b. These steps in total, with their separate types of relevancy, cover all that is pertinent to the profitable growth of the business.

    c. Their sequence and content progressively narrow the areas of information and decision.

    d. Their sequence and content indicate significant relationships between the information, judgments, and decisions of any one of them with the information, judgments, and decisions of all the others.

6. *Does the process invite or minimize duplication of planning effort?* Obviously it should and will minimize effort if—

a. The process directs effort to only relevant matters.

b. Wherever similar information is used in more than one step, it is the same information previously obtained or the same information extended in form or substance.

c. The process builds on previous judgments and decisions with each progressive step.

d. It calls for individual, nonduplicating contributions from each function and from general management based on the particular capabilities, perspective, and responsibilities of each.

e. The process requires that information, judgments, and decisions be recorded in such a manner as to minimize the effort needed to understand and use them in planning and its execution throughout the business.

7. *Does the process invite its application by those having the most knowledge of a subject and discourage its use by others?* Conscientious application should reveal quickly what is and is not known concerning matters essential to the profitable growth of the business. It ought to show superficial knowledge, judgments, and decisions in their true light and thereby demand the attention of those who have the necessary knowledge or who are responsible for obtaining it.

8. *Does the process encourage the development and consideration of alternative courses of action?* The particular sequence of the process described here, plus the participation in it of all functional areas, is designed to elicit for full consideration all the alternatives possible under the circumstances known and anticipated by anyone in the business.

9. *Is the written record of the output of the process—*

a. *In simple form for use by the planners?* A record in "chapter and verse" by important subject matter is called for.

b. *In a form which will spotlight the sources of warnings that further planning—or changes in present planning—may be required?* The suggested critical conclusions and assumptions concerning needs, customers, and competition cover these sources outside the business; measurement of progress against timed results covers those within it.

c. *In a form that can be conveniently modified and updated?*
Organization by chapter and verse permits partial modification of planning without revision of the whole.

d. *In a form that will aid precise measurement of progress?* Mileposts are required along the road of each opportunity—objectives and targets—against which integrated progress in all areas of the business can be measured.

e. *In a form to simplify communication throughout the business?*
Communication will be effectively streamlined if the discipline of the process as to substance is observed and if the suggestions as to form and use previously outlined are followed.

PART THREE:

Organization and Control

The form of any organization is dictated by the kind of work to be performed in terms of expected results. It is from this basic reference point that major organization problems must be considered and the roles of corporate planning, corporate marketing, and other staff units determined. The fundamental principles are generally applicable to a wide range of businesses, both large and small. Worth particular attention are the positions of marketing manager and product manager, the marketing research activity, and the contributions of research and engineering.

12. Organization for Customer-Oriented Planning

PREVIOUS CHAPTERS HAVE EXPLAINED HOW PLANning for the business operation as a whole evolves from integrated planning by all its functions, and how it can and should lead to true customer orientation. Within this framework there should be planning by every organizational unit and every individual in the business. The kind and amount of planning done, the degree of dependence upon planning for the business as a whole, and the value of the contribution made will vary widely depending upon the basic organization structure assigned responsibilities and authorities.

There are any number of ways in which one can effectively organize to operate a business. These different ways are suggested—and, in some instances, required—by the nature of the business. The basic form of organization may depend, for example, on whether the business is a selling or a manufacturing operation, whether it involves more or less technical capability, and whether it serves consumer or industrial markets.

No attempt will be made here to explore the different organization structures and all their planning; the range of possibilities is too great. The suggested business planning process should provide considerable direction and guidance for anyone interested in specifying the form which planning activity is to take in any organization unit, or any position, in a particular business. Some additional guidance is provided by certain organization principles and positions which have general application. Perhaps the most important of these—and certainly one that is most commonly overlooked—holds that the form of organization is dictated by the kind of work to be performed in terms of expected results.

It is no happenstance that the term "organize" follows the term "plan" in the often-repeated definition of the managerial function: that is, "to plan, organize, integrate, and measure." One must organize to do what is planned. Carried to its logical and practical conclusion, this means that one cannot organize without first planning what is to be accomplished. In business, one should no more organize for organization's sake than one should plan for planning's sake. Neither is intended as an entertaining exercise for jaded executives. Both are sharp tools for conscientious stewards to whom have been assigned valuable resources for use in the service of people's material needs.

ORGANIZATION AT THE COMPANY LEVEL

A business, then, cannot organize any activity properly before it knows what that activity is supposed to accomplish. Therefore, it cannot properly organize for planning until it has determined what is to be accomplished by this activity and what is involved in its accomplishment. If the planning process outlined in this book is adopted by a business, it will require organization along certain lines, and it will rule out organization along other lines. Some of the organizational features it requires have already been indicated. Others will be mentioned in the course of a quick look at some organizational aids to planning first at the company level and then at the level of operating divisions within the company.

The Corporate Planning Unit

There is currently a very popular organization unit at the company level which is not compatible with the suggested business planning process. This is the unit or position established, and supposedly given full authority and responsibility, to plan for the business as a whole—but not for the operation of the business. It has found considerable acceptance with big companies which can afford it and which have complex and widespread planning and operating problems. It is sometimes called "corporate planning."

The head of a business who feels the need for help in planning, and therefore establishes such an organization unit or position as his right hand, may, however, be creating rather than solving a problem. This will almost inevitably be true unless he fully understands his problem and is guided accordingly. What is his problem?

Whenever the top executive, because of the complexity and sheer size of his operation, feels that he wants some sort of assistance in coping with his planning responsibility for the business as a whole, he is not looking for someone to take over and do his job so far as it relates to planning. If he were, he would be seeking his successor—for, as previously explained, a most important part of his contribution to company management in general and planning in particular is decision making on the basis of the recommendations made to him. Nor is he looking for someone to perform the roles in business planning which should be assumed by the respective functions. If he were, he would in effect be replacing those functions. Rather, the top executive in these circumstances is seeking someone who will—

1. First in point of time and importance, determine what particular planning process is most suitable for the business.
2. Upon his approval of the process, install it throughout the business by explaining it and assisting in its application.
3. Assist him in his personal participation in business planning by gathering information and offering judgments and recommendations for general management decisions concerning purpose, scope, and strategy.
4. Prepare the statement of business planning and, after he has made the decisions upon which it is based, keep it up to date.
5. Assist him in evaluating the output of this planning, and in measuring progress against planned results, by organizing and applying review and evaluation procedures.
6. Develop and communicate new knowledge concerning improved techniques for business planning.

7. Develop and implement improved techniques for evaluating business planning efforts by all participants.

In effect, the head of the business in these circumstances is establishing a position or an organization unit to serve some of the personal needs which he has as general manager. When these needs are identified as such, the proper scope of the organization unit in question can be clearly defined and understood by everyone throughout the business. In any event, it should be made exceedingly clear that this unit has not been delegated the authority and responsibility of the general manager for the decision making required by business planning, nor the authority and responsibility of all operating and functional units for their respective forms of participation. Except for one-man operations (which can't afford the luxury of such a position or unit), no single individual or small group of men can have the knowledge, or the time, to do all that the business planning process implies—especially for a large corporation. Furthermore, to the extent this deficiency in knowledge and time could be corrected, manpower and abilities would be duplicated and line authority and responsibility would be confused and emasculated.

The far too prevalent misinterpretation of the relationship between budgeting and planning has led some companies to assign the responsibility for corporate planning, however defined, to the financial area. In this connection the findings and observations of E. Kirby Warren again are revealing and persuasive.

The confusion between budgeting and planning is unfortunately quite common, and the result is most undesirable. If planning and budgeting are viewed as being virtually synonymous, then major portions of the planning responsibility, including much implied objective setting and program design, may be turned over to the "budgeteers"—men whose financial accounting background often has not prepared them to carry out complete planning jobs.

Budgeting is, after all, largely the translation of objectives and programs into financial form. To turn over major portions of the responsibility for planning to budget specialists is like turning over major portions of the responsibility for international policy making and speech writing to the technicians at the United Nations who translate such statements into other languages.

In annual planning, this abandonment of responsibility for objective setting and program design is somewhat less critical, since much short-term planning is really little more than the allocation of available resources within the framework of existent policy. But for the elements of current decision making that must reflect change in policy because of environmental changes, and for the aspects of longer-range planning that are designed to alter the company's course, planning must go beyond the limits of the budgeteer.

Budgeting and financial accounting activities constitute only one aspect of long-range planning, but it is an important aspect. The primary function of the budget group is the translation of plans into financial terms. Although many of the financial implications of various objectives and programs are self-evident, a second function of the budget and accounting group is analyzing financial plans and reporting to management on the less obvious indications. A third and related group of responsibilities involves working with division officers to help them achieve their desired goals along desired lines, but in such a way as to produce better-balanced and more desirable financial results.[1]

Mr. Warren seems to concur in recommending the role of corporate planning advocated here, for he says:

> The director of long-range planning is not so much a planner as he is a supervisor and coordinator of planning. He will be called upon to advise on planning, but his principal responsibilities are to direct and coordinate its conduct.
>
> . . . There are instances where the division manager or corporate officer who makes the appointment is actually far from convinced that long-range planning is worth the trouble. Where this is the case, formal long-range planning is almost certainly doomed to ineffectuality.

Participation by Other Staff Units

Whenever a business is so complex and big as to require a unit of the kind described, it may also require other staff positions or organization units. How do these other units participate in planning, and what is their proper relationship to the corporate planning unit or position?

To explain by example, let it be assumed that a business has three

[1] "Where Long-Range Planning Goes Wrong," *Management Review*, May 1962, pp. 4-15.

decentralized operating divisions. Each has its own general manager and separate organizations to perform all the functional activities required for these profit centers. The general managers report to the president, as do half a dozen staff units. Included among these are corporate planning, corporate finance, corporate research, corporate engineering, corporate manufacturing, and corporate marketing.

The role of corporate planning has already been suggested. If it is adopted, the three operating divisions and the staff units will look to corporate planning for the development of basic business planning procedures. These will include procedures for planning the operations of the company as a whole and the activities of each operating division as individual businesses. In other words, corporate planning might establish a business planning process like the one recommended in this book; each operating division would then follow the process and develop a statement of business planning for itself. Further, each function in each operating division would develop its own statement of functional planning.

The business planning process, or the basic planning procedure, specifies the kind of contribution which each function must make to planning for the business as a whole, but it does not spell out in detail how each function is to make that contribution and complete its functional planning. The other staff units should therefore be sources of knowledge about improved planning techniques. Corporate finance should have responsibility and authority for determining what financial planning procedures are required by the company, and will be most suitable for it, within the basic framework of the established business planning process. Upon executive approval of these financial procedures, corporate finance should install them throughout the company by explanation and assistance in applying them within each operating division. Corporate research should have similar responsibility and authority for planning procedures in its area of specialized knowledge, as should corporate engineering, corporate manufacturing, and corporate marketing.

But, even when all the operating divisions have applied the business planning process in full and have statements of business planning supported by statements of planning for all functions, the necessary planning has not yet been completed, even temporarily.

There is still some planning work to be done for the company as a whole—work which involves more than merely adding up and summarizing the planning outputs of the three operating divisions.

If each of these divisions has done a good planning job, it has related the assigned, available resources to customer needs within its scope. No attempt should have been made at this operating level to relate other resources of the company to other customer needs. These other resources are of two kinds: those which are a combination of all the resources assigned to the operating divisions and those which have not been assigned to any of them. Significant combinations of technical skills or production capacities typify the first. A new material or process which is developed by the company's research and development unit, and which is foreign to any of the operating divisions, is an example of the second. The other customer needs also are of two kinds: those which are within the scope of the company but have not been assigned to any operating division, and those which are not within the scope of the company.

Information, judgments, and recommendations concerning these matters cannot and should not be developed by the operating divisions but are the province of the staff units. They call for application of the business planning process at the company level—initiated by corporate marketing with each of the other staff units participating and contributing according to its function. The president will of course make the general management decisions which are required, and corporate planning will be responsible for assisting him.

The output of such planning at the company level should be consolidated with the output at the operating division level in a "Company Statement of Business Planning." The format for this statement will be the same as that used by the operating divisions and outlined on pages 170-171. In content, it will summarize the output of divisional- and company-level planning in a manner that will be most meaningful to the president. Corporate planning will prepare and maintain this statement. For reasons already noted, participation by all the staff units is important, and the role of corporate marketing is critical.

If corporate marketing is to measure up to this responsibility, provision must be made organizationally for the planning work required. It would be impossible here to cover all the facets of this problem; in brief, however, a position or unit should be organized within corporate marketing with responsibility and authority to—

- Identify any customer needs which could be served by the company but which are not within the scope of any operating division.
- Ascertain the product and service requirements of such needs.
- Evaluate company and competitive capability relative to these requirements.
- Determine the nature and magnitude of the opportunities connected with the needs.
- With others in corporate marketing, utilize this information in developing recommendations as to which opportunities so identified should be pursued and with what strategy, objectives, and targets.

This position or unit will be predominantly concerned with work leading to the planning of new products for the company. For that reason it might be labeled "corporate marketing–product planning"; however, it will be more appropriate to describe it as "corporate marketing–customer requirements." For, while corporate marketing will be responsible for recommending targets—some of which will concern new products—corporate research, corporate engineering, and corporate manufacturing will be actively involved in the planning of those products. Whatever it is called, performance in this position or unit will lean heavily on the assistance of marketing research, provision for which should be made either in corporate marketing or elsewhere.

ORGANIZATION AT THE OPERATING DIVISION LEVEL

This business planning process also assumes or requires certain forms of organization in the operating units. To sum up: It proposes a basic organization structure along functional lines. It suggests that one of these functions be called marketing and that it include important planning responsibilities in addition to sales, advertising, and others long recognized. How should marketing be organized so as to do this planning most efficiently?

Since the primary direction for organization comes from the kind of work to be performed, this question can best be answered by starting with a definition of marketing's role in the business in terms of expected results pertaining to planning. These results may be stated as follows:

1. Complete, communicated knowledge concerning the situation of the business; that is,

   a. *Needs*

      (1) The particular needs which could be served.
      (2) Their magnitude (past and future).
      (3) Their product and service requirements.
      (4) Basic methods of service (past and future; relative magnitudes).

   b. *Customers.* Who has these needs; their profiles, problems, and so on.

   c. *Competition.* Who else can serve these needs; their profiles.

   d. *Economic, social, and political factors.* Which ones affect the situation (past and future); nature of their impact.

2. Complete, communicated knowledge of the *resources* of the business from a marketing standpoint; that is, resulting capabilities as related to product and service requirements.

3. Complete, communicated knowledge of the nature and magnitude of all *opportunities.*

4. Sound recommendations (based on 1-3 above) concerning

   a. Suggested business *strategy.*

   b. Suggested *volume, profit, and market position objectives* for the business.

5. Sound recommendations concerning

   a. Major action programs *(targets)* throughout marketing to support individual objectives.

   b. Major action programs to maintain and develop marketing resources required in connection with all opportunities.

6. Efficient implementation of all marketing programs approved by general management (including organizing, integrating, measuring, and performing the activities required).

7. Efficient, continuing marketing planning to develop current infor-

mation, judgment, and recommendations of the kind described in
1-5 above.

From the standpoint of the general manager and the other functional managers of the operating divisions, the marketing manager is
responsible for accomplishing these results. To them he is the "marketing planner" referred to in our explanation of the business planning process. Under some circumstances, as will be explained later,
he may delegate a portion of this responsibility for certain products
or product lines; but under all circumstances he, as the marketing
planner, is responsible to the business as a whole and should participate in the planning process personally. In fact, planning should be
one of his major activities.

In this marketing planning activity, the marketing manager will of
course require the direct assistance of all the key people in his organization and the indirect assistance of everyone in marketing. He must
organize within marketing so as to tap the knowledge and judgments
of all regarding situation and resources. For example, headquarters
and field sales can and should contribute substantially in this respect.
He must also organize so as to have the benefit of recommendations
relative to proposed strategy, objectives, and targets from those in
marketing who are directly and intimately involved and most knowledgeable concerning different aspects of these planning elements.

The particular way in which the marketing function should be
organized to require such full, across-the-board participation in marketing planning will vary with the size and basic organizational structure of the particular business. The possibilities are too numerous
for exploration here. However, there are two positions in marketing
which are found, in one form or another, in many marketing organizations and which are particularly important to planning.

Marketing Research

Wherever it may be in the business, at a staff level or within an
operating division, marketing research is a tool for marketing management. In essence, its role is to bring to marketing management
the scientific approach to fact gathering and analysis with respect to
all problems in marketing, whether they concern planning, organization, integration, or measurement.

More particularly with regard to planning, this role of marketing research—like that of marketing planning itself—can perhaps be best understood in terms of the results it is expected to contribute toward that planning. With brief notes on the procedures involved, these are:

1. *Results relative to need*

    a. Proficient assistance to marketing management in the *identification of basic demand* and its elements.

    Upon request, marketing research analyzes the relationship of a particular product to the basic demand in connection with which it would be purchased and the relevant segments of that demand. (See Chart VII, pp. 78-79, and the discussion in Chapter 4.)

    b. Complete, communicated knowledge of the *general magnitude* of that basic demand and its segments, past and future.

    Upon request, marketing research determines general magnitude for the past on the basis of secondary data, and for the future on the basis of judgment, taking into account trends and economic, social, and political factors.

    c. Complete, communicated knowledge of the past and future *magnitude of each need* specified by marketing management.

    Upon request, marketing research determines past magnitude on the basis of secondary data, and future magnitude on the basis of judgment, taking into account trends and economic, social, and political factors.

    d. Complete, communicated knowledge of *data external to the company* concerning any details designated by marketing management relative to product and service requirements.

    Upon request, marketing research obtains any available marketplace data indicative of what may be the practical ideal requirements from the customers' standpoint.

    e. Proficient assistance to marketing management in determining the past and future *relative magnitudes of the basic methods of serving each need.*

    Upon request, marketing research determines the basic methods of serving each need in the past; their relative magnitudes; the economic, social, and political factors which may affect these basic methods in the future; and their probable impact.

2. *Results relative to customers.* Proficient assistance to marketing

management identifying all customers and their problems and profiles as directly related to each need.

Upon request, marketing research determines what classes of customers have had the specified need in the past; their total demand; those of their problems and profiles as a class which are directly related to the need; the economic, social, and political factors which must be taken into account; and the probable nature of the impact in the future on these classes of customers and their demands, problems, and profiles.

3. *Results relative to competition.* Proficient assistance to marketing management in identifying all competitors with their market shares and profiles in serving each need.

Upon request, marketing research determines what classes of competitors have served the specified need in the past; their strengths and weaknesses in that service; the pertinent economic, social, and political factors; and the probable nature of the impact in the future on classes of competition and their market shares.

4. *Results relative to economic, social, and political influences.* Complete, current, communicated knowledge of these factors and the nature of their impact on specified needs in the past and their probable future impact.

Marketing research organizes and records the information and judgments described in 1-3 above in such a manner as to convey a clear understanding of them to marketing management and to permit their ready modification in the future in accordance with actual developments.

5. *Results relative to resources.* Complete knowledge of the marketing research resources required for the successful operation of the business.

Marketing research determines what resources it has available and what will be required in the future to accomplish effectively the results expected of this activity. Upon approval of marketing management, it develops and maintains these resources.

6. *Results relative to opportunities.* Complete, communicated knowledge of the past and future magnitude of opportunities identified by marketing management.

Upon request, marketing research provides marketing management with a written statement of the historical record and projected future magnitude, in units or dollars, of all such opportunities. The resulting information and judgments should have the same form and content as developed under 1-5 above, although in some instances reorganization may be required to conform to the opportunities as identified and measured.

7. *Results relative to marketing research targets.* Complete com-

municated knowledge of any major marketing research programs required to support marketing objectives.

Marketing research recommends to marketing management any major marketing research activity needed to support objectives for each opportunity.

8. *Results relative to special studies.* Complete, communicated knowledge of marketplace data as may be requested by marketing management from time to time to aid in evaluation of any action program under consideration.

Upon request, marketing research obtains whatever marketplace data are available and relevant to specified action programs and communicates this information in the most meaningful and succinct form.

9. *Results relative to execution of marketing research programs and studies.* Competent execution of all required marketing research programs and studies in keeping with developing circumstances.

Marketing research plans and organizes to carry out these programs, integrates their performance with other related activities in marketing, and periodically measures their progress and effectiveness.

10. *Results relative to continuous marketing planning.* Continuing contributions to marketing planning in the manner described above.

On a continuing and systematic basis, marketing research updates information and judgments called for in 1-6 above.

Marketing research obviously has a vital role to perform in marketing planning and business planning. The rewards are rich for those who recognize, organize, and utilize this activity properly. Management must take great care to avoid the extreme practice, common in many businesses today, of either assigning the function an "ivory tower" status in which it devotes itself to sheer statistical analysis or making the marketing researcher a mental alter ego and ghost writer for members of management who are unwilling or unable to do their own planning. As this outline of expected results will indicate, the marketing research man is supposed to be far more than the source of neatly compiled statistics: He must make certain projections which are basic to all the business's planning. These may be modified through the refining of the planning process, but they are critical to thinking and decision making in all the areas of the company.

Marketing management is, however, responsible for these projections in two respects. First, it defines what projections will be made by identifying the particular needs that are of interest to the company. Second, marketing management decides whether these projections are adequate for marketing planning purposes. The knowledge and judgment of marketing management therefore represent an important additional ingredient.

Product Manager

In many cases, the scope of the business is such that broad and diverse product or market areas may be involved. Under these circumstances it is often deemed advisable to assist the marketing manager by assigning certain marketing management responsibilities to several men, reporting to him, called product managers. Whenever this is done, these product managers should be the primary "marketing planners" with respect to their individual lines and the customer needs which are thereby served. Of course, their planning is subject not only to the approval of the marketing manager but to such modification as may be required by his planning for the business as a whole. The marketing manager therefore retains his responsibility for marketing planning aimed at the service of all needs: those assigned to the product managers and any that are not assigned. So far as the assigned needs are concerned, the respective product managers have the same kind of relationship with marketing research as the marketing manager himself.

Within the marketing function, the most important positions with respect to marketing planning are the marketing manager, the marketing research man, and—where he exists—the product manager. This does not mean that others in marketing do not make vital contributions to this planning. They do. Just as the business planning process calls for efforts from the bottom up and from the top down, as well as from all the functional areas of the business, so the procedures within marketing should call for each subfunction's participation. To this end, the marketing manager and/or product managers should first outline—in writing—situation (with the assistance of marketing research), resources, scope, and purpose. To these should be added a description of the nature and magnitude of all the opportunities which the marketing manager (or product manager) sees plus his thinking on strategy. He should submit this information for review and suggestions by all the subfunctions: sales, advertising, and the like. The subfunctions should then offer any corrective or supplementary information and judgments from their respective standpoints and make recommendations as to strategy, the selection of opportunities, and proper objectives and targets for each.

In this manner, through the continuing interchange of information, judgments, and recommendations, the marketing manager can develop what he will finally offer to the other functions of the business as the frame of reference for their contribution to business planning.

ORGANIZATION FOR RESEARCH AND ENGINEERING

A great deal of attention, in this and previous chapters, has been given to the marketing function. Two facts explain and justify this emphasis: (1) That function does not seem to be understood fully in theory or practice; and (2) the effective performance of marketing activities is critical to sound business planning and the customer orientation of the business.

One of the basic requirements for this customer orientation, as we know, is the express assignment to the marketing function—and its complete fulfillment—of the responsibility for keeping general management and the functional areas informed concerning customer needs which could be served by the business and for recommending how they should be served. Another such requirement, however, is similar effectiveness on the part of the research and engineering function(s) in the assigned area of responsibility and authority: the development of new or improved products and processes for the better service of identified and selected customer needs.

The responsibility of research and engineering for technical developments in processes and products which will lead to reductions in costs and improvements in current product quality seems to be clearly recognized and generally understood. Activities in these areas of specialization directed toward such ends are accordingly guided with some appreciation of their significance to the business. The responsibility for technical developments which will lead to new products also is clearly recognized but less specifically understood in most businesses. Therefore, activities designed to encourage new product development usually are either too much or too little; it may be open to question whether they are of the right kind and emphasis. The responsibility for fundamental research, on the other hand, seems to be only vaguely recognized and understood except in those businesses which consider such research to be the major or secondary service they offer to customers.

Since organization for research and engineering should, as with any other areas of specialization, be dictated by the kind of work to be performed in terms of expected results, thinking should start with some analysis and consideration of the organizational problem from that standpoint.

Relationship with Marketing

The work to be done by research and engineering in terms of expected results for the business as a whole has already been stated: "to develop improved and new products required for the better service of identified and selected customer needs." One way in which these needs can be identified and selected has been described. Chapter 8 gives the role and the expected contributions of research and engineering in some detail. It is there suggested, by implication at least, that the relationship between marketing and research and engineering is most important. Since this is so, and since that relationship appears to be less understood than that between these functions and manufacturing or finance, let us first direct our attention to that relationship as it affects the business as a whole.

What are the basic facts about the mutual interests and related activities of these areas of functional specialization? First, each R & E project has some significance from a marketing standpoint. Dealing as it does with product, process, or knowledge, it therefore also deals with resources. It can affect existing resources or create new ones, both of which are available for serving customer needs and must be related to needs by marketing.

Second, the degree of marketing significance varies according to the possible impact on specific opportunities. Changes in research or engineering resources can lead to greater or less capability for serving certain customer needs. A project's significance is partly established by the extent of the change in capability which flows from it. However, one cannot fully evaluate that significance to the business as a whole without relating such capability to particular customer needs and without knowing how important those needs and the resulting opportunities are to the business.

For example, new or increased knowledge concerning the properties of a material used by the business in manufacturing a product may open up several possibilities. The quality of the old product may be improved, leading to greater customer acceptance. Or the cost of the old product may be reduced, leading to either a reduction in price or more profit, or both. The old product may in fact now have several more uses in serving new customer needs. All the opportunities so created are probably not of equal importance to the business. Some may be big, others small. Some may lead to growth in profit or volume; some may not. Some may support the strategy of the business; some may not.

Again, the true worth of any business resource should be more than its intrinsic value. Only through its contribution to serving particular customer needs, within scope, and in a manner consistent with purpose and strategy, does it attain full value.

Third, the precision with which such marketing significance can be determined depends upon the completeness of our knowledge concerning what specific effect the project will have on resources, how the resulting capability of the business as a whole can be utilized in serving particular customer needs, and with what results for the business. Thus we recognize the dual, interrelated kinds of uncertainties which must be resolved. What does the business have, and how can it be used for profitable growth? In this respect a business is like a man playing five-card stud poker. He contributes to the pot before being given a hole card and must ante up again before being given subsequent cards.

A business makes its first contribution by its initial investment in R & E manpower and facilities. The continuation (or expansion) of that manpower and those facilities and the application to specific projects constitute the payments to be made before the second, third, fourth, and fifth cards are dealt. Like the player, the business must evaluate its hand before each ante: what is in it, what it might become with additional cards, and what the chances are of winning the pot. That evaluation, on the basis of the first two cards, is of necessity far more speculative than it should be after four or all five cards have been dealt. In business as in poker, there is a series of evaluations, each of which should be more complete and refined as new information (or cards) is available.

The business's organization and procedures should assure this series of evaluations for each R & E project from its inception and throughout its existence. The series should be so designed that the business can with progressively increasing confidence determine, at any stage before making another ante, whether the stakes and the risks are worth further investment. Like the poker player, management cannot be sure even with the most complete and refined information and judgment that it will win. A business must, however, take calculated risks.[2]

Fourth, marketing significance is a factor which should be considered in establishing, guiding, measuring, and planning for all R & E projects. If, over the long term, these do not pay off in profitable service of customer needs, there will be no funds with which to conduct research and engineering. Fifth, there is the question of technological significance; projects are required and undertaken only because of some desire for more technological knowledge. Sixth, significance in this respect will depend upon the area of technical knowledge concerned and the possible contributions to it.

Some knowledge is gained in every research and engineering project even though no solution may be found to the question which prompted it. In business, however, some areas of technical knowledge are more important than others because of the particular scope of the company. Also, some contributions to technical knowledge are more important than others because they lead more directly to, or have a greater impact on, efforts to accomplish the purpose of the business. Under certain circumstances, developing a new product may be more important than reducing the cost of an old one, and vice versa. Relative importance can be established only by an evaluation from the standpoint of the business as a whole.

Seventh, fundamental research projects should be planned, undertaken, guided, and measured primarily on the basis of their possible

2 The appropriateness of this poker-game analogy is confirmed by its use in Quinn, James Brian, and James A. Mueller, "Transferring Research Results to Operations," *Harvard Business Review*, January-February 1963, pp. 49-66.

technological significance. Fundamental and basic research is original exploration for the advancement of scientific knowledge; it is not directed toward a specific product or process. Of course, such other factors should be considered as technical feasibility, availability of funds and manpower, and, if at all possible, marketing significance. Projects should, however, be limited to the areas of knowledge which are currently of technical significance to the business. This principle recognizes the responsibility which the director of research, like all other functional managers, has for maintaining and developing the resources assigned to him. He must undertake certain projects of a fundamental nature from time to time, but in doing so he must keep in mind his companion responsibility for the optimum utilization of all resources to achieve the company's purpose. It is possible, for a short time, to maintain and develop resources without applying them to the service of a particular customer need. It is not possible, however, to utilize them fully in any other way.

Eighth, all other research and engineering projects should be planned, undertaken, guided, and measured primarily on the basis of their marketing significance; again, technical feasibility, availability of funds and manpower, technological significance, and the like are secondary considerations. The rationale for this assertion has been succinctly stated by Harold O. Ladd, manager, Marketing Research Division, Development Department, E. I. du Pont de Nemours & Company, Inc.

> The unfilled needs of consumers, whether industrial or public, are marketing facts—actually the most basic—whether recognized or not. However, unfilled needs require definition and measurement before they can be considered from a commercial standpoint. Thus the ideal time to begin the appraisal of those needs is at the time or before commitments are made for technical study. The reason for this is that research and development are expensive, and hundreds of thousands of dollars may be spent only to come up with a product which has little, if any, commercial significance. If we can avoid this pitfall through the early accumulation of marketing information, we may save or at least restrict expenditures which otherwise represent a direct drain on profits.[3]

[3] From an address given before the Annual Spring Meeting of NAM's Marketing Committee, Rye, New York, May 1-2, 1958. See "What Modern Marketing Means to Corporate Success," *Current Issues Series*, No. 2, Economic Problems Department, National Association of Manufacturers, pp. 18-21.

Three Categories of Work

The first seven principles, with the related reasoning, should lead us logically to the eighth, which is also substantiated by the broad classification of research and engineering work in three categories according to the kind of results desired:

1. R & E projects designed to *maintain or develop current resources.* All fundamental and basic research projects should fall in this category and should be governed by the seventh principle.
2. R & E projects concerning means which will enable the business to *satisfy better, or more profitably, certain customer needs that are currently being served.*
3. R & E projects concerning means which will enable the business to satisfy *certain customer needs not currently* being served.

These last two categories presuppose the identification and evaluation of particular customer needs in terms of their possible contribution to the profitable growth of the business and the kind of product required to serve those needs. They should therefore be governed by the eighth principle.

The marketing significance of projects in the second category may be fairly obvious to everyone in research, engineering, and, in fact, all the other areas of specialization, since only currently served needs are involved. For example, a project addressed to a specific improvement in product quality in answer to numerous customer complaints requires little explanation of its marketing significance. However, an improvement in quality which is not prompted by complaints, but is suggested by a determination of product and service requirements and could lead to a new class of customers, calls for full explanation if its significance to the business as a whole is to be understood by all concerned. And, since the third category includes only projects related to needs which are not currently being served by the business, it is most unlikely that anyone in the business will be aware of their true importance unless and until their marketing significance has been determined.

The marketing function (at company and operating division

levels) should identify customer needs and provide the basic frame of reference for their consideration by all other functions (see Chapter 8). Research and engineering should expect and demand full information as to the marketing significance of any projects falling into these last two categories. Even though, initially, this may not be precisely determinable, the guidance provided should favor an earlier and more profitable payoff than would otherwise be possible. Furthermore, that guidance should be progressively more precise as the project develops.

These principles—particularly the last—are not intended to suggest even by implication that projects in research and engineering are initiated only upon the request of marketing. If marketing lives up to its responsibilities as recommended in this book, many research and engineering projects will be prompted by its findings, conclusions, and proposals. Also, by determining and communicating the product and service requirements of particular needs, marketing suggests the direction which product development should take and may even request specific product improvements or developments to support sales programs. However, research and engineering can and should initiate projects on their own. The point is simply that no project—other than fundamental and basic research—should be carried on without prompt and progressive measurement of its marketing significance.

Expected Results

In brief, the role of research and engineering within the business might be described in terms of these expected results:
1. Efficient planning and execution of such fundamental and basic research projects as may be required to maintain and develop those technical resources which are most significant to the business from a technological standpoint.
2. Effective communication with all functional areas of the business (particularly marketing) so as to keep them currently informed of the technical resources of the business, including those under development or in prospect; recommendation of their optimum utilization by the business.

3. Sound recommendations concerning suggested business strategy, volume, profit, and market position objectives, within the basic frame of reference initiated by marketing in the consideration of all the opportunities available to the business.

4. Sound recommendations concerning such applied research and engineering projects as are required to support the strategy and the volume, profit, and market position objectives of the business; and, upon general management approval, proficient execution of those projects.

There are basic procedures for the business as a whole which are necessary to the efficient functioning of research and engineering. Included are specific evaluation techniques and checkpoints for three kinds of research and engineering projects: product, process, and fundamental. All exemplify the customer orientation approach and planning process from which they are derived.

13. General Management Evaluation and Control Of R & E

THE TREMENDOUS INCREASE IN THE EXPENDITURE OF research dollars by American business over the past 15 years is clear proof that people are fully awake to the great contribution that can be made by this area of specialization to the profitable growth of many businesses. But this awareness is not enough; it is only the beginning. Systems must be devised to harness this great potential or, from a business standpoint, more will be lost than gained.[1]

The first requirement is that the role of research, within the business as a whole, be recognized. This we have outlined and briefly explained. The second requirement is the adoption of basic procedures for the business as a whole which will permit and facilitate the proficient execution of that role.

The procedural suggestions which follow assume a business which is manufacturing and selling certain products. It is organized along functional lines, with separate research and engineering, marketing, manufacturing, finance, and law activities. For simplicity's sake, research and engineering projects are considered under three headings:

---

[1] See Drucker, Peter F., "Twelve Fables of Research Management," and Quinn, James Brian, and James A. Mueller, "Transferring Research Results to Operations," both in *Harvard Business Review*, January-February 1963, pp. 103-108 and 49-66, respectively.

Reference No. _____
Evaluation No. 1 2 3 4 5 6

FORM I
(Master Sheet: Page 1)
EVALUATION
of
PRODUCT RESEARCH AND ENGINEERING PROJECTS

RESEARCH AND ENGINEERING

Date _____

Kind and nature of improved or substitute product expected from project (however, if the product idea originates in some function other than R & E, responsibility for specifying the kind and nature of the product shall rest with the originator and this source must be indicated):

Nature of research and engineering work involved:

Estimated time required:

MARKETING

Date _____

Potential	Historic Record Current 195_ 195_ 195_ Year 196_ 196_ 196_ 196_
Need	
Opportunity (units-$)	
Company volume (present product)	
Market position (present product)	

Possible effect on opportunity: *Possible effect on company volume:*
☐ Maintain size   ☐ Maintain volume
☐ Increase size   ☐ Increase volume
   ☐ Major ☐ Minor   ☐ Major ☐ Minor

Key assumptions regarding product features reflected in marketing evaluation:

Recommendation:
         ☐Cancel project   ☐ Evaluate further

1. *Products projects.* Those whose goal is a new, improved, or substitute product. This category includes projects directed toward processes and materials leading to such products.
2. *Process projects,* including those directed toward new or modified methods, machinery, or materials, with no new or modified product intended.
3. *Fundamental and basic projects.* Those whose goal is the discovery of new principles—an increase in the body of technical knowledge—for utilization in applied research and engineering (that is, product or process projects).

PRODUCT PROJECTS

Product projects must relate either to an opportunity which is now being pursued by the business or to a new opportunity. Each will be considered.

R&E Projects Related to Opportunities Now Being Pursued

The goal here is an improved or substitute product for one now offered to customers. Projects should be identified and evaluated by means of a sheet like Form I. Instructions for its use follow:

Step 1. The project should be identified in general terms by research and engineering, but must include the nature of the product improvement or of the kind of product expected.

If this is a new project, whoever is requesting or sponsoring it should write the description.

Step 2. The "nature of research and engineering work involved" and "estimated time required" should be stated by the research and engineering personnel concerned.

Step 3. The balance of the first page of the form, following the heading "Marketing," should be completed by interested marketing personnel (marketing manager or product manager).

If marketing finds that further exploration is not necessary because the volume and market position possibilities are either adverse or negligible, R & E should be so informed and the project should be dropped. In all other instances, further, more complete evaluation is necessary along the following lines.

Reference No. _____

Evaluation No. 1 2 3 4 5 6

Date _____

FORM I

(Page 2)

MARKETING SECTION

Need, opportunity, company volume, market position (past and
projected with improved or substitute product):

Desirable production date:

Price considerations:

Special marketing activities required:

Nature

Risk of accomplishment (or area of uncertainty)

Time required

Cost estimate

Impact on and from:

Prices or volume of other products

Previously scheduled marketing work

Previously evaluated marketing programs still under consideration

Important marketing resources

Other important marketing considerations:

Step 4. As soon as possible after a project is recommended, marketing must estimate what effect it might have on volume and market position (see Chapter 7). Marketing's estimates should be progressively sharpened with time and developments. Initially, the business has no choice but to rely on the estimate of marketing, even if it is only an educated guesstimate.

Marketing will develop the best possible original estimate and progressively refine it by organizing its thinking, findings, and conclusions as indicated on Form I (Page 2), Marketing Section. At whatever time (or times) it is completed, it should be attached to the sheet previously described, thereby becoming the second page of that master form.

If marketing has prepared a "Statement of Marketing Planning" of the form and content previously recommended, and is maintaining it currently, the task of completing Page 2 of Form I in connection with opportunities now being pursued should be relatively simple and quick. Needs and opportunities have already been identified and measured; company volume and market position objectives have been established; supporting action programs and strategies have been planned in marketing. The only question is what changes in these should result from successful completion of the project under consideration. And marketing has the basis on which to make an informed judgment.

After this judgment of marketing has been recorded, Form I—with the marketing section attached—should be returned to research and engineering. This second look by R & E is designed to permit a careful, complete evaluation from the technical standpoint, which would have been unnecessary if the initial screening by marketing under Step 3 had proved negative.

Form I (Page 3), Research and Engineering Section, guides this more complete evaluation and provides a means for recording the technical considerations most significant to the business as a whole and communicating them to others. The sheet should not be difficult to complete if research and engineering has developed and maintained a statement of planning as previously recommended.

Upon completion of this evaluation, Form I—with the marketing and research and engineering sections attached—should be turned

(text continues on page 211)

Reference No. _____

Evaluation No. 1 2 3 4 5 6

Date _____

FORM I

(Page 3)

RESEARCH AND ENGINEERING SECTION

Particular research and engineering activities required:

   Risk of accomplishment (or area of uncertainty)

   Timing and cost estimate

Impact on and from:

   Budget

   Previously scheduled R & E work

   Previously evaluated projects still under consideration

   Important R & E resources (for example, manpower, facilities, know-how)

Other important research and engineering considerations:

Reference No. _____

Evaluation No. 1 2 3 4 5 6

Date _____

FORM I

(Page 4)

MANUFACTURING SECTION

Particular manufacturing activities required:

Nature

Risk of accomplishment (or area of uncertainty)

Time required

Cost estimate

Impact on and from:

Previously scheduled manufacturing work

Previously evaluated work still under consideration

Important manufacturing resources

Other important manufacturing considerations:

Reference No. _____

Evaluation No. 1 2 3 4 5 6

Date _____

FORM I

(Page 5)

FINANCE SECTION

Special expenditures:

    By periods of time

    By individual functions

    Total

    Effect on budgets of each function

Effect on financial resources:

    Cash flow

    Profit

Other important financial considerations:

Reference No. _____

Evaluation No. 1 2 3 4 5 6

Date _____

FORM I

(Page 6)

LEGAL SECTION

Patent implications:

☐ Patentable

☐ Patent infringement

General comment

Legal implications:

Recommendations:

Reference No. _____

Evaluation No. 1 2 3 4 5 6

Date _____

FORM I
(Page 7)

GENERAL MANAGEMENT SECTION

☐ Further evaluation required

☐ Cancel project

☐ Suspend project

☐ Proceed with project   _____ Progress review date

Reasons and conditions (including relationship of project to strategy and company objectives):

over to manufacturing. This function records its evaluation and recommendations in the manner indicated in Form I (Page 4) and attaches the sheet to the master set.

The finance function can now intelligently estimate what financial results and problems can reasonably be anticipated from the project under consideration. A sheet like that shown as Form I (Page 5) can be used to guide and to record the evaluation process.

Master Form I—with the sections prepared by marketing, research and engineering, manufacturing, and finance attached—should be reviewed at this point by the company counsel. His evaluation might be recorded as suggested by Form I (Page 6) for incorporation with the rest.

With the addition of this last functional section, Form I is ready for review by the general manager. His decision can be meaningfully recorded and communicated to all the functional areas of specialization by use of suggested Form I (Page 7). Copies of this section should be given to all functions.

If it is decided to proceed with the project, the general manager should set the date for a progress review—certainly no later than one year ahead. Immediately prior to that review, Form I should be updated by the functional areas in the sequence previously outlined —with a report on progress and on any change in program. Here, in short, we have

Step 5. This process should continue throughout the life of any project, until both the project and its results have been formally and fully incorporated in the statement of planning for the business as a whole and those of the different functions. Each project should be so incorporated as soon as possible.

R&E Projects Related to New Opportunities

In this case, the goal is an improved or substitute product for a new end use or for new customers. The same basic procedures and forms apply to this type of project. However, since we are concerned here with new opportunities, we will not have available data and previous marketing planning on whose basis marketing projections and judgments can be readily made for Steps 3 and 4. For these new opportunities marketing should in effect combine Steps 3 and 4, noting on the Master Sheet, Page 1, *only* "Key Assumptions" and

"Recommendations." Initial marketing estimates and information set forth in the Marketing Section (Page 2) will therefore be less precise and more subject to progressive refinement in time; that is, during Step 5 of the evaluation process.

PROCESS PROJECTS

Projects in this category are directed toward new or modified methods, machinery, or materials, with no new or modified product intended. They are primarily conceived in hopes of improving cost, quality, or both. While they may have a great deal of marketing significance and may be specifically prompted by product and service requirements, it is neither desirable nor possible to bring marketing's evaluation into the picture as early as with respect to product projects.

Form II can be used for these projects. It is initiated by research and engineering. Upon completion it should be passed on to manufacturing, which will record and attach a manufacturing section as shown in Form II (Page 2). The financial evaluation will be next, covering at least the points in Form II (Page 3); and, then, a legal section should be added as in Form II (Page 4).

All these first evaluations are designed to determine the impact of successful completion of the process project on the company's internal functioning; for example, ease and cost of operations. One more perspective is necessary. What impact can be expected from the customers' standpoint, and how can it be utilized? For example, can and should price be changed?

Marketing's evaluation should be guided and recorded as shown in Form II (Page 5). Now Form II, with the attached sections from research and engineering, manufacturing, finance, law, and marketing, is ready for review and decision by the general manager, who will record and communicate this decision on a sheet resembling Form II (Page 6).

FUNDAMENTAL AND BASIC PROJECTS

Fundamental and basic projects, as stated, are directed toward the discovery of new principles and are intended to increase technical

(text continues on page 220)

Reference No. _____
Evaluation No. 1 2 3 4 5 6

Date _____

FORM II

(Page 1)

EVALUATION
of
PROCESS RESEARCH AND ENGINEERING PROJECTS

RESEARCH AND ENGINEERING SECTION

Nature of process improvement (expected results):

Nature of research work and engineering involved:

Estimated time required:

Risk of accomplishment (or area of uncertainty):

Cost estimate:

Impact on and from:

    Budget

    Previously scheduled R&E work

    Previously evaluated projects still under consideration

    Important R&E resources (for example, manpower, facilities, know-how)

Other important research and engineering considerations:

Reference No. _____

Evaluation No. 1 2 3 4 5 6

Date _____

FORM II

(Page 2)

MANUFACTURING SECTION

Particular manufacturing activities required:

Nature

Risk of accomplishment (or area of uncertainty)

Time required

Cost estimate

Impact on and from:

Previously scheduled manufacturing work

Previously evaluated work still under consideration

Important manufacturing resources

Other important manufacturing considerations:

Reference No. _____

Evaluation No. 1 2 3 4 5 6

Date _____

FORM II

(Page 3)

FINANCE SECTION

Special expenditures:

By periods of time

By individual functions

Total

Effect on budgets of each function

Effect on financial resources:

Cash flow

Profit

Other important financial considerations:

Reference No. _____

Evaluation No. 1 2 3 4 5 6

Date _____

FORM II

(Page 4)

LEGAL SECTION

Patent implications:

☐ Patentable

☐ Patent infringement

General comment:

Legal implications:

Recommendations:

Reference No. _____

Evaluation No. 1 2 3 4 5 6

Date _____

FORM II

(Page 5)

MARKETING SECTION

What specific opportunities can be affected by accomplishment of the project?

What is the past and projected magnitude of each such opportunity and of company volume, market position, and profit—with and without the improvement?

How will the improvement be utilized by marketing to obtain these results?

Other important marketing considerations:

Reference No. _____

Evaluation No. 1 2 3 4 5 6

Date _____

FORM II

(Page 6)

GENERAL MANAGEMENT SECTION

☐ Further evaluation required

☐ Cancel project

☐ Suspend project

☐ Proceed with project   _____ Progress review date

Reasons and conditions:

Reference No. _____

Evaluation No. 1 2 3 4 5 6

Date _____

FORM III

EVALUATION
of
FUNDAMENTAL AND BASIC RESEARCH PROJECTS

DIRECTOR OF RESEARCH

Area of technical knowledge and its importance to company technological resources:

Nature of research involved:

Proposed time and manpower:

Estimated cost:

Impact on and from:

   Budget

   Previously scheduled R&E work

   Previously evaluated projects under consideration

   Established R&E budgets

General comment:

knowledge with a view to its utilization in applied research and engineering. Therefore, they are activities designed to maintain and develop the technical resources of the business.

As pointed out in Chapter 12, it is seldom possible to relate these projects quantitatively to specific opportunities. Evaluation and control of fundamental and basic research projects must of necessity rest primarily with the director of research and the general manager. Suggested Form III may be useful. On this basis, and guided by his own vision of the future, the general manager can decide how much he wants to invest in fundamental and basic research. His vision will be considerably sharpened if the entire business is customer-oriented and its planning operates along the lines suggested.

* * *

James Brian Quinn, under a grant from The Alfred P. Sloan Foundation, Inc., made a two-year study of planning for research and development, in the course of which he interviewed more than 120 top research, operating, and planning executives. In a subsequent article based on that study,[2] he addressed himself to the question: What part should top managers play in the research planning process? Mr. Quinn's major findings and conclusions, as related to this book's theme, can be summarized under the points below. Following each point is a brief, parenthetical comment cross-referencing it to the theory and procedures previously recommended.

1. Establishment of key company objectives is the first step in the process of total planning for research.

    R&D planning cannot be sound without the direction provided by company objectives. However, these cannot be conceived by top management in abstract and handed down. Rather, they must be developed from below, starting with the business planning process. R&D should contribute to their development and be guided by them in their tentative and then their final form.

2. Overall objectives help to define the scope, degree, and timing of the company's technological requirements. Without these, R&D drifts toward studies which fascinate individual scientists, the pet projects of executives, short-run sales, and other activities which bear little relation to long-term requirements.

---

[2] "Long-Range Planning of Industrial Research," *Harvard Business Review*, July-August 1961, pp. 88-102.

This is true with respect to all the functional requirements of the company, not just R&D.

3. Mere statement of objectives is not enough. All key decision makers must understand these objectives and act in concert to realize them.

   This is one of the reasons why objectives must be stated in writing and communicated to all concerned. Company objectives are focal points for the integration of all functional and profit center objectives.

4. A company must make certain decisions before it can set its objectives. These concern:

   - The business the company wants to be in. This must be defined in terms of the nature of the goods or services the company wants to produce rather than the means of providing those goods or services. To stimulate creative research a look should be taken at the functions the products are to perform.

     Scope should be defined in terms of the needs to be served. Customer needs are defined in functional terms.

   - General objectives which aren't related to capabilities are meaningless guides to research planning.

     Timeless intentions (purpose) are helpful in determining what kind of results are desired for the company. On that basis the company must establish objectives (timed results) which management expects to achieve *with its capabilities*. Objectives can be properly developed only by identifying needs and opportunities and relating to them all resources.

   - Direction of intended growth, such as vertical integration or horizontal growth.

     Determined through strategy.

   - Method of growth intended. If growth through research is intended, the whole posture of the company must be adjusted accordingly.

     Developed and directed through strategy.

   - Desired company image, technologically.

     Developed and reflected through strategy.

   - Research programs are stimulated or restricted by other factors such as the desired size of the company, the percentage of the market to be held, the kinds of markets the company wants to compete in, and the desired rate of return.

     Each opportunity must have its own specific objectives as a foundation for planning and achievement in all functional areas of the business, including research. Each research program, other than fundamental and basic projects, should be evaluated relative to specific opportunities.

5. Most long-range top management decisions do not require pinpoint decisions in projections. As the future unfolds, early decisions can be modified, nullified, or reinforced.

Reflected in theory and procedure.

6. A company should be interested in all possible technology which will impinge on the needs of its present and potential customers.

The business planning process requires knowledge of all means of serving customer needs and projections of their future development. Research personnel should supply knowledge to marketing and refine and enlarge the knowledge made available by marketing.

7. Three general environmental projections are needed for long-range research planning: economic, social, and technological.

Economic, social, and political factors and technological developments are all covered in situation, but they must be pinpointed to needs, customers, and competition. Otherwise the information is too general for everyone, including research.

8. Research must be responsive to technological knowledge from three sources: (*a*) the scientific community in general, (*b*) the company's present and prospective customers, and (*c*) the company's competitors. Mathematical formulas are almost worthless in technological forecasting. The requisites are human judgment, knowledge of the scientific field under study, a real sense of the economic implications of science, and imagination.

The business planning process calls for marketing to initiate the basic frame of reference within which research and all other functions develop, from their respective standpoints, all possible substantiating and modifying information. Research should draw heavily on the three sources.

9. The first reading of the general scientific environment can be gained by looking at published information concerning current development programs. The second reading is obtained through determination of what society will require in the future on the basis of social and economic developments.

This approach is right in principle but somewhat broad in application. Product and service requirements must be developed to bridge the gap between economic generalizations and specifics. A third reading can be had by assessing the impact of fundamental research programs—an assessment which can be made only by knowledgeable scientists.

10. A company can gain much knowledge through consultation with the customers' technical personnel.

Such consultation is more meaningful if it has the focus of product and service requirements.

11. The mission of research must be defined carefully by management.

    The mission of research is broadly established by company scope, company purpose, and company strategy; it is specifically defined by tentative objectives and targets for specific opportunities proposed by marketing, confirmed or modified by research and the other functions, and finally approved by management.

12. Management must define what research is to contribute, not how that contribution is to be made.

    This principle is reflected in the suggestions concerning the process for business planning and the procedure for evaluation and control of research and engineering projects.

13. Research strategy should indicate when and where to (*a*) concentrate research efforts, (*b*) remain "on the grapevine" with the scientific community, or (*c*) virtually ignore developing technology. A company must first saturate its "bread and butter" field with research programs. Second, by projecting customer technological needs and competitive programs, it must determine the likeliest areas for heavy development and applied research. Third, management must determine how to look at its particular strengths and weaknesses where the optimum technological opportunities exist.

    Marketing should provide the basic frame of reference within which the company can determine (*a*) technical feasibilities and (*b*) strengths and weaknesses as compared with those of competition.

14. No one has a real formula for determining "just the right amount" to spend on the entire R&D program. The most prevalent and successful approach is individual program analysis, with other criteria used only as a general check on judgment. Individual program analysis builds a program from the bottom up by ranking each project on the basis of how well it will fulfill company desires.

    This is preferable to the "top down" approach and is provided by the business planning process and its supporting R&E project evaluation procedures.

15. R&D projects must be selected in such a way as to provide an integrated research program. This can be done in three planning steps:

    • In the case of *present products,* a prediction of potential market must be obtained for each product class. This will mean assessing what technology will be required to keep the product attractive and safe from inroads of substitutes.

In determining situation, we decide the magnitude of the need and product and service requirements for each and all opportunities.

Gaps must then be identified by comparing present with needed technology. If enough technical information is available to fill these gaps, only applied research programs are necessary. If enough information is not available, fundamental research programs are required.

A look at product and service requirements indicates gaps, and research objectives and targets should be established to fill them. These gaps should provide specific direction for applied research projects but only general guidance for fundamental and basic research.

- In the case of *foreseeable new products*, the first thing to do is to find new market applications, estimate their size, determine what technology is needed, and decide whether there are any gaps. Applied and fundamental research must then be planned accordingly. Again, planning new lines first identifies market needs and then works back to sequential programs which will meet these needs.

  In determining situation, the magnitude of the needs is arrived at; then, by looking at the product and service requirements, new opportunities are identified.

- For *entirely new applications* see below.

16. Fundamental research is a fountainhead of technology for new applications beyond those presently foreseen. The planning process is here reversed: technical planners must identify scientific areas with promise but without direct relationship to known needs. Ultimate decisions on this element of the R&D program must be left to trained scientists.

    Reflected in the evaluation procedure for fundamental research projects.

17. Specific criteria for evaluating each individual R&D project stem from considerations in each functional area.

    Reflected in R&E project evaluation procedures.

18. General management must rely on scientific skill to assess technical feasibility. But a function of nontechnical management is to insure that project selections are adequately tested against company goals and that all relevant business considerations are weighed in project decision.

    Reflected in R&E project evaluation procedures.

19. A procedure should be established in each company for review of projects at all organization levels. Nonresearch **members should**

raise probing questions to keep research on its toes and in tune with company goals and technological needs.

Reflected in R&E project evaluation procedures.

20. As a last step in program development, top management should step back and take an objective overall look at the package of projects it is supporting.

     Specific criteria will be provided by a statement of overall business planning.

21. Involving operating personnel in R&D planning and review will increase understanding of research progress and prepare the way for the transfer of research technology into operations. Optimum results can be achieved only when research is properly integrated into the company's overall planning.

     Reflected in the business planning process and the R&E project evaluation procedures.

With James A. Mueller, under a grant from the McKinsey Foundation for Management Research, Inc., Mr. Quinn has since concluded another study which called for interviewing more than 200 top operating and research executives in the United States. On the basis of their accumulated experience, Messrs. Quinn and Mueller offer a four-step program for improving the flow of technical innovation from research to operation.[3] They recognize that no single solution to the problem is best for all businesses, but they have found that the following four kinds of management action do stimulate that transfer. Again, there are parenthetical comments relating their thinking to the recommendations made in this book.

Step 1. "Examine resistance at critical technological transfer points." In the typical large company there is a complex of several technological flows: between specialized areas within research, between decentralized units, between functional areas (such as marketing, manufacturing, and finance), and between organizational levels. A clear understanding of the relationship between technology *producing* and technology *using* must precede the design of a sound transfer system.

The business planning process ideally is based upon such an understanding and reflects it.

Three things must be transferred across each flow point: (*a*)

[3] See "Transferring Research Results to Operations," *Harvard Business Review,* January-February 1963, pp. 49-66.

information about technology, (*b*) enthusiasm for technology, and (*c*) authority to use it. Many varied barriers exist for each.

Step 2. "Provide the information to target research" through a "company-wide long-range plan" and, in addition, "adequate commercial information to rank and balance R&D programs to meet company goals." This additional information requires "three major types of information-generating functions":

- "Opportunity seeking," concerned only with new opportunities.
- "Commercial intelligence," concerned only with "present and potential competitors' commercial and technical activities."
- "Economic-evaluation functions" suggested by "opportunity seeking," by new R&D technologies, or otherwise.

Targeting R&D will be vastly improved if management gives adequate attention to the following factors:

- "Management must assign the responsibility for providing opportunity-seeking, commercial-intelligence, and economic-evaluation information to specific competent groups."
- "The company must develop a procedure which forces periodic evaluation of each R&D program in terms of the best available information concerning its commercial implications and technical feasibility."
- "The information must actually be used by top technical and business managers—not as rigid bench marks, but as guides in the exercise of mature judgment—to determine which R&D programs should be further emphasized, cut back, or eliminated."
- "Infeed information must be presented in a way which researchers can understand and which motivates them to work on problems significant to the company."

The suggested business planning process, supported by the recommended procedures for evaluating R&E projects, takes into account all these considerations. The previous organizational and procedural suggestions do not, however, contemplate three separate and distinct information-generating activities and, presumably, three different organization units to perform them. These activities are blended together and performed at both company and operating division levels. (See Chapter 12.)

Step 3. "Foster a positive motivational environment."

- Through a *policy and executive attitude* "which encourage flexibility, reward . . . successful change, and promote cooperation between organization units."

The suggested business planning process, supported by the recommended procedures for evaluating R&E projects, permits as well as promotes cooperation.

- Through *control on the basis of long- rather than short-term goals, results, and rewards.* The overuse of short-term control is considered to be "the most significant single factor contributing to negativistic motivational environment."

The recommendations in this book are all designed to force a long-term orientation to all aspects of business management.

Step 4. "Plan and control exploitation of R&D results."

- Through *specific formal organizations* with authority to carry a new technology to commercial success and to force line organizations to give it attention.

Procedural and organizational recommendations here are directed to this end, particularly those concerning the customer requirements position at both company and operating division levels. (See Chapter 12.)

- Through *formal transfer procedures* which assure programs planned from research to exploitation and controlled throughout with progressive evaluations.

The recommended procedures for evaluating R&E projects provide for progressive programing, evaluation, and control superseded by incorporation into the business planning process.

- Through the *examination of critical strategies* dictating how and when different transfers should be made.

The business planning process and the related evaluation procedures for R&E projects are designed to force development and application of strategy for the business as a whole and for each functional area of specialization. Thus they cover both technology-producing and technology-using areas.

How can management determine the extent to which a business has become customer-oriented? How it can become more so? These are questions which suggest an obvious need for specific standards and checkpoints.

14. Criteria for Evaluating Customer Orientation

CUSTOMER ORIENTATION IS THE AWARENESS, AND fulfillment, of the concept that the profitable growth of a business depends upon its future ability to serve selected customer needs rather than sell particular products or services. It is evident through attitudes and conditions both in and outside the business. Alert management will want to evaluate periodically the degree to which true customer orientation has been attained, and pinpoint areas for possible improvement in this respect.

Evaluation of Internal Attitudes and Conditions

Here are suggested criteria, with brief explanatory notes and checkpoints, for evaluating attitudes and conditions inside the organization.

1. Is the concept of customer orientation understood, accepted, and communicated by management as a way of business life?

    Note: The president establishes company environment and attitude. A general manager establishes operating division environment and attitude.

    Checkpoints: Statement of company purpose. Company policies. Other formal expressions by management at all levels.

2. Is the scope of the company, and that of each operating component, based upon the particular customer needs to be served?

    Note: No one can serve all customer needs. Each business should concentrate on those needs for which it has particular capabilities.

Checkpoints: "Scoping" by definition and assignment of specific customer needs, not just facilities. Recognition of present and changing capabilities.

3. Have responsibility and authority been assigned to the marketing function, clearly and expressly, for identifying customer needs which could be served, keeping general management and all functional areas informed concerning them, and recommending how they should be served?

Note: Adept performance of sales, advertising, and other marketing activities depends upon various kinds and amounts of detailed information. In addition, marketing—as the company's eyes and ears in the marketplace—must keep general and functional management informed of key market factors which should affect their decisions and action. These key factors are:

- The customer needs which are being served, and which could be served, by company products.
  a. By individual opportunities related to particular products or product lines;
  b. In terms of their anticipated nature and magnitude over at least the next five years; and
  c. In terms of "ideal" functional, appearance, economic, and service requirements from the standpoint of all customers.

- The customers who have, and will have, these needs.
  a. Their type, classification, and location; and
  b. Their problems and the opportunities associated with these needs.

- The competitors who are serving, or could serve, these needs.
  a. According to their methods of service;
  b. In terms of comparable past and anticipated ability to serve them; and
  c. In terms of their anticipated strategies and programs.

- The capability of the company.
  a. By functional area and in total; and
  b. As related to the above.

Checkpoints: Definition of marketing function. Qualified personnel. Appropriate procedures for obtaining and disseminating the information outlined as market factors.

4. Have responsibility and authority been assigned to the research and engineering function, clearly and expressly, for developing improved and new products required for the better service of identified and selected customer needs? And are all research and engineering projects—other than fundamental and basic—progressively evaluated from the standpoint of their marketing significance?

Note: R&E's responsibility for cost improvement projects is well recognized and controlled. However, R&E projects for new and improved products should be so guided that they will be addressed to the particular customer needs which offer the best opportunities for the company.

Checkpoints: Definition of research and engineering function. Procedures for evaluation of individual R&E projects by all functions, beginning with marketing.

5. Are all functions of the company so organized as to permit their full participation in the recommendation of those opportunities associated with identified customer needs which should be pursued— and how? Have they been provided with adequate communication systems and procedures?

Note: "All functions" includes marketing, R&E, manufacturing, finance, law, etc. The systems and procedures should be directed toward the development of joint recommendations for general management consideration and decision.

"Opportunities" covers those now pursued and those which are new.

Checkpoints: Organization charts. Definition of functions. Communication systems. Procedures for evaluation of opportunities.

6. Are all functions of the company concerned for, and do they understand, the *product and service requirements of each customer need served*? Do they understand company capabilities in relation thereto?

Note: Product and service requirements represent the main vehicle by which marketing conveys understanding of a particular customer need to R&E, manufacturing, and finance. If these functions, and marketing, concentrate on these requirements and fully utilize all the company's capabilities to satisfy them better than the competition, the company will be trying to satisfy *customer* rather than *company* problems— whether they concern performance, appearance, delivery, price, or whatever.

Checkpoints: Definition of product and service requirements by marketing. Utilization by all functions with understanding of company resources.

7. Are business decisions and strategies concerning needs to be served and the method of service based on 3, 4, 5, and 6? Are they made with due consideration for long-term as well as short-term implications?

Note: Are all action programs and strategies proposed and considered within the frame of reference provided by the information specified in 3 above and the specific results to be achieved in terms of volume, market position, and profit? Are all general management decisions made only after consideration of all available information and recommendations of the kind described?

Checkpoints: Memoranda recommending management decisions. Minutes of decision meetings.

8. Are these business decisions concerning needs to be served and methods of service expressed as objectives—directly or indirectly related to volume, market position, and profit—against which performance is measured throughout the company?

   Note: Does management quantify its decisions by specifying expected results? Are the action programs contemplated by these decisions actually directed and measured by these objectives?

   Statements of planning should spell out the objectives and supporting action programs in all functions. For example, in the marketing statement the sales programs and supporting advertising should be directed specifically to the need being served, the customers having that need and their problems—not just to the selling of a product. (This applies to field as well as headquarters sales.)

   Checkpoints: Statements of planning, business and functional. Their use in directing and measuring progress.

9. Does the company have adequate organization and procedures to provide the foregoing information, recommendations, decisions, implementation, and measurements in the future—on a current and continuous basis?

   Note: General management is concerned with the present and the future but can influence only the future.

   Checkpoints: All listed above.

Evaluation of External Attitudes and Conditions

Criteria for evaluating attitudes and conditions outside the company can be summarized in the same way.

1. Do most presently served customers believe that the company fully understands—or is conscientiously trying to understand—the particular needs being served and is trying to supply products and associated services which will satisfy the requirements of those needs more quickly and satisfactorily than its competition?

   Note: Full understanding requires knowledge of the functional, appearance, and economic requirements of the need from the standpoint of all customers—those to whom the company sells and their customers, down to and including the ultimate user.

   Checkpoints

   • Opinion of customers' purchasing staff, based upon degree of *a.* Continuous company field sales order solicitation and order service in terms of product and service requirements of needs and field sales inquiries and interest concerning customers' future needs, their product and service requirements, and the company's relative capability thereto.

      b. Periodic company headquarters sales and management solicitation, inquiries, and interest of the kind described above.

- Opinion of customers' research, engineering, and manufacturing personnel, based upon degree of

      a. Continuous company field sales interest in current and anticipated customer problems involving technical matters which can be affected by company products or services.

      b. Prompt and effective technical assistance through the company's research, engineering, manufacturing, and customer services organizations in solving technical problems associated with company products.

- Opinion of customers' financial staff, based upon degree of

      a. Continuous company field sales interest in customers' financial status and full utilization of company terms and financial arrangements.

      b. Equitable and reasonable application to customers of company's policies concerning terms and financing.

- Opinion of customers' marketing personnel, based upon degree of

      a. Continuous company field sales interest in customers' current and prospective marketing problems which can be affected by company products or services.

      b. Periodic company headquarters sales and management inquiries and interest concerning customers' profitable growth possibilities and the company's possible contributions thereto with its products and services.

2. Do most potential customers believe that if the company served them, it would fully understand—or conscientiously try to understand—the particular needs being served and would make every effort to satisfy the requirements of those needs more quickly and satisfactorily than its competition?

   Note: Today's potential customer can be the key to the future.

   Checkpoints: Opinion of potential customers' purchasing, research, engineering, manufacturing, finance, marketing, and management personnel, based upon knowledge of others' experience with the company in any or all of the respects outlined in connection with External Criterion 1.

3. Do most competitors consider the company a leading and successful originator of products and associated services which win customer acceptance?

Note: A company that keeps offering customers something new which they accept is consciously—or otherwise—oriented to their needs.

Checkpoints: Attitudes and imitative actions of competitors.

4. Does the company have a reputation in business circles generally for broadening old and developing new markets—not just fighting over a share of existing markets?

   Note: Customer needs and their satisfaction are dynamic rather than static.

   Checkpoints: Opinions of competitors and business and investment leaders, based upon their knowledge of company actions and public statements (including advertising) concerned with customer rather than company problems and accomplishments.

Customer orientation, plus a sound planning process, has a positive, personal impact upon the individual. This is true at all levels and in all areas of specialization. And the most important resources of the business—time and manpower— are thereby developed and enhanced.

15. Meaning for the Individual

WHETHER OR NOT TIME, STRICTLY SPEAKING, IS the most important resource of a business, it—of all resources—cannot be replaced. Moreover, anyone arguing its claims to first position would certainly agree that manpower is the next most important. And, since manpower is the only means of saving and utilizing time for the benefit of the business, we might reasonably conclude that it tops the list. In any event, we can safely assume, as managers and planners, that time and manpower are our two most valuable assets; no basic orientation and procedure, such as the suggested business planning process with its organizational and operating implications, should be adopted without measuring the probable impact on these resources.

Some reference has been made in previous chapters to the effect of this process on time. Customer orientation and business planning focus on the future—the only aspect of time which is available for use by the business. They require anticipation of future events, thereby leading to advance preparation and, hence, better utilization of time. The planning process forces early judgments and decisions and permits easy modification to suit changing circumstances. It develops the relative importance of individual opportunities to the business and thereby permits the proper allocation of time and other resources to their pursuit. Finally, it provides a more factual and reasoned basis for assuring timely action by management as related to customers and competition.

The business planning process as described here is time-consuming for everyone involved, particularly in its inception. However, the time will be well spent; and, with experience, much less time is consumed and a great deal is saved. Even the original application of the process should require considerably less time than is now wasted in the fruitless conferences between functions with which management too often attempts to cope with planning and programing in bits and pieces.

Security—or Security of Opportunity

But what do customer orientation and the planning process mean to the individual? They can and should constitute a giant step toward giving him that which he most desires—*security of opportunity*.

Our country was founded and has grown to its present world status on the basis of this desire, articulated and satisfied in many different ways in different phases of life. Until recently, however it might be expressed in a man's business life, it was a challenge easily accepted and easily fulfilled. Today we find many in the American business community preoccupied in thought and deed with security alone.

In the long run, however, security in any form must be earned, it cannot be given. Attempts to bestow it contain in themselves the seeds of growths which can choke and destroy it. Throughout history, treaties and pacts have failed to make weak nations secure. In the business arena, security arrangements by way of legal (or illegal) agreements between different companies have never been successful, in the long run, for all involved. Aside from legal considerations, it is naive for an American businessman to think he is providing for the security of his business by entering into pricing agreements with his competitors. In effect, he is trying to take a short cut which, in time, will weaken the ability of that business to survive. Perhaps he hopes he will not be around when the piper must be paid.

This preoccupation with security is a slow rot so far as individual development and strong individual character are concerned. It spreads with each increase in pay and fringe benefits which is unrelated to increased productivity—both in the white-collar and hourly wage ranks and at managerial and supervisory levels. The true source of increased pay and benefits—and, therefore, security—is increased productivity of the business generally, which depends upon the increased productivity of every individual in it. Some of the suggestions in this book, it is hoped, will lead to increased productivity on the part of managers, supervisors, and professional employees. If this almost virgin territory for improvement is tapped, perhaps better solutions will be developed for accelerating the rate of increase among rank-and-file workers and for apportioning to customers, employees, and stockholders alike the benefits of greater productivity.

True Meaning for Individual Jobs

No man can increase his productivity unless he at least knows what his job is and what its standards are and unless he has some incentive for superior performance.

In spite of all the seeming advance in the science or art of management, American business appears to grow less rather than more adept at meeting these minimum requirements for employees—particularly white-collar workers. Surely the answer to this basic problem will not be found through the development, in abstract, of still more sophisticated organization charts, job descriptions, time and motion study techniques, communication systems, wage and salary programs, bonus and incentive systems, and profit-sharing programs. Rather, this and many other basic management problems can be solved only if American business understands and successfully grapples with the fundamentals of business life as they are discussed here.

How can a business give true meaning to managerial and other jobs unless it has more than a superficial understanding of the information, judgments, and decisions required by the planning process? Without a full understanding, even the head of the business cannot really know his job or the standards of performance required of him. Without the assistance of sound information and judgments, he cannot perform his unique function properly; he must abdicate rather than delegate. In most cases a careful analysis will reveal that if a general manager has a material incentive for superior performance, it is only remotely related to increased productivity on his job. And such conditions are not fair to him or to the business.

Bruce Payne has suggested that "long-range planning is a discipline which is almost incompatible with the temperament of the American business executive." In explanation he says:

> The very qualities which have gone into making the American business executive fight against the fact finding and analysis of planning. No executive likes to feel that he is creating a super structure "plan" which will discipline and limit his freedom of action as he moves forward over the next years. . . .
>
> The key executive in any organization is not a man who does things by rote—he does not react to preassembled facts and plans as an automaton or robot. Rather, he is usually an individual *passionately* desirous of controlling his own destiny; he is creative, imaginative, and he hates to be second-guessed. This executive fights control, and he does not seriously believe that there are many outside influences and pressures either now or in the future which can limit him, if he has the sheer will and desire to grow and move forward.

Mr. Payne then concludes:

> Planning will sell itself to top management when two goals are achieved—when there is better, more imaginative planning and when our key executives—in fact, our companies and our American economy as a whole—achieve a higher level of self-discipline. . . .
>
> If your plan includes imaginative and creative forecasting, a keen awareness of corporate strengths and weaknesses, and if you set your objectives high enough so that they stretch your corporate fiber to meet them, even the most creative executive will find himself with *a dynamic and powerful company to work with.* The discipline involved will become the means for achieving the aspirations of the individuals associated with the company, rather than limiting these aspirations.[1]

The Real Measure of Success

How can a director of research really know his job and the standards of performance which must guide him without the kind of orientation provided by the planning process? If he is a true professional, as he should be in his position, he undoubtedly will understand the technical content of his job. But what about the business content? How can he increase his productivity if he doesn't know

[1] From an address at MacKay-Shields Associates, Inc., Long Range Planning Forum, New York City, October 13, 1960.

what specific contributions he can make to the profitable growth of the business? How can his performance be fairly measured?

The research activity should be an incubator of new resources for the business. From an operating standpoint, these—like other resources—have no intrinsic worth. They acquire full value only through their proper utilization in serving some particular customer need in a manner consistent with the purpose of the business. Most research people in industry realize that if their projects do not, over the long term, pay off in profitable service of needs there will eventually be no funds with which to conduct research. Therefore, a research man cannot establish, guide, and evaluate the progress of individual projects without some understanding of how the resources to be developed may possibly be utilized and what their significance to the business is likely to be.

By its very nature, a fundamental or basic research project cannot be related to a specific customer need. It can, however, be related broadly to the preservation and enhancement of "the state of the art" in those fields which are most important to the business—provided these are known. And such knowledge can be gained through careful application of the planning process.

All other research projects can be related to the service of particular customer needs. The resources to be affected or created will open possibilities of serving needs not served before or of serving—better and more profitably—those needs already being served. In the beginning, this relationship can be perceived only in general terms. However, as a project continues, it can be determined with increasing precision.

From the standpoint of the business and its profitable growth, it is imperative that the research activity, in general and in terms of individual projects, be related as specifically as possible to the payoff in the marketplace. From the standpoint of the director and that of his associates who are assigned to particular projects, it is equally imperative. The planning process offers a procedure not only for determining this relationship but for giving the research activity a direct role in establishing objectives and programs for the utilization of developed resources by the business as a whole. Thus research becomes a full-fledged member of the management team and a basic procedure is provided whereby real meaning, from a business standpoint, can be given to individual research positions. What better way is there to destroy the frustration which feeds on wasted efforts? What better way is there to generate enthusiasm in truly creative individuals?

Stimulus of Personal Satisfaction

With only minor modifications these same comments apply to other company functions. Take the people in engineering, for example, ranging from the director to the engineers assigned to specific projects. In business circles, one often hears references to an "engineering monument" or "white elephant." How can engineers be blamed for these follies if they are not oriented to the marketplace? In the absence of proper guidance, they naturally apply their full effort to the engineering content of their jobs.

Through customer orientation and the planning process, the engineers in a business are provided with information about the marketplace which permits them to channel their creative talents in the right direction. It both permits and requires their participation in establishing what can and should be done by the business in the service of customer needs. As they work on a project, they have more than a vague idea of its importance. When they are successful, their sense of accomplishment is heightened by the awareness of what it means to the business. This personal satisfaction is one of the most powerful and neglected forces for increased individual productivity in business today—particularly *big* business. Engineers and research personnel, because of their nature and their work, are even more responsive to this sort of stimulation than some of their associates in other functions. As a general rule, however, they are permitted this self-satisfaction only in the case of major accomplishments on which they have received little or no guidance from marketing and other company groups.

Of necessity, the manager of manufacturing and his associates are accustomed to planning ahead. Manufacturing facilities cannot be built, or planned, overnight. Even relatively minor modifications are more long-term than short-term in nature. With accelerated progress in automation and the increasingly complex problems connected with direct labor which are bound to result, the need for sound long-range planning by manufacturing will grow rather than diminish. Nor can this planning be done in abstract.

Manufacturing's basic aim is to produce the kind of products, at the times and in the quantities required by the customer, in the most proficient manner possible from the standpoint of the business. How can anyone in manufacturing accomplish this to his own satisfaction or that of his associates if customer requirements are not anticipated with some degree of certainty and if plans in all areas of the business are not integrated on that basis?

The thrill of satisfaction which manufacturing people naturally get from a newly constructed factory with the most up-to-date equipment is replaced by bitter resentment and frustration if that factory efficiently turns out a good product which is not of the kind, or in the quantity, required by customers. Substantial over- or undercapacity is, of course, a major problem for everyone in the business, but its impact is greatest on manufacturing. Customer orientation and the planning process provide means whereby capacity can be geared more closely to customer needs and to the ability of the business to serve them. Today some industries are obviously suffering from overcapacity and others are facing that possibility. Would they—and all the companies and individuals involved—not benefit from customer-oriented planning?

In most businesses, the manager of finance and his associates have long been recognized as more than recorders of financial results and custodians of the cash box. Among other things they usually participate actively in any planning for the future. They estimate costs and profits, prepare budgets, and make arrangements for any financing that may be necessary. But on what basis? Past experience? Judgment? Vision? All of these—and more—are required of the financial man from his particular vantage point.

The financial man's task is difficult enough when he has all the tools required for his trade; he should not be asked to work with only a crystal ball. It is unreasonable, from his or the business's standpoint, to ask that he guess what marketing, research, engineering, and manufacturing will do and with what results in the future. Nor is it fair to ask that he take bits and pieces of information from each area, wholly or partly unrelated, and make a sound estimate of future costs, much less future profits. The planning process will provide him with the information and judgment that he needs from other areas of the business.

The Salesman of the Future

Customer orientation and the planning process obviously have particular meaning for people in marketing. There is, for example, the salesman, who is too important to be treated—even by implication—as the forgotten man.

The day of Arthur Miller's Willy Loman and even of his more up-to-date counterpart is over in more ways than one. Today's and tomorrow's circumstances require and are developing a new kind of salesman. He must still be an expert in persuasion and maintain close personal contact with his customers; however, he must utilize this talent and this contact for more than just today's sales. His responsibility is essentially one of building the strongest possible relationship between his company and his assigned customers with a view toward their mutual growth. In this context he must know what needs these customers have which can be served by his company; the performance, appearance, and economic requirements of those needs; the shortcomings of his and his competitors' products in satisfying those requirements; and the importance of the needs to the future of the customers. On the basis of his knowledge, and under his leadership, his company must determine to what extent it is capable of serving the needs and then undertake to do so in a manner which will be profitable for both parties.

To his customers, the successful salesman of the future will be an individual personification of the customer-orientation concept. He will be the field extension of the headquarters marketing function. He will perform in miniature, for assigned areas in Customer Land, the planning and execution required of marketing. He will draw upon and contribute to headquarters planning. He will be able to plan and operate on the basis of his own situation, resources, scope, purpose, opportunities, strategy, objectives, and targets. When all this comes to pass, the salesman's job—by whatever name it is called—will make its rightful contribution to the business and offer true security of opportunity.

Eugene B. Mapel, vice president and director of marketing services for the Chase Manhattan Bank, suggests:

Many top managements . . . are aware that their salesmen are no longer able to sell with only a persuasive demonstration of their product's functional superiority. They know that the salesman must be a "resource manager" who must invest corporate resources other than his own time and selling skill in a profitable way. They expect this. They demand it. But many of them have responded by only demanding. . . .[2]

The difference between the old and the new role of the salesman, with its challenge and prestige, is clearly outlined by Carl Rieser. As examples of companies that have recognized this new role, he cites General Electric, Texas Instruments, Kimberly-Clark, FMC, General Foods, Du Pont, Allis-Chalmers, IBM, National Cash Register, and others. He concludes with this statement:

The trouble is that business has signally failed to get across the idea that there has been a tremendous change in selling. Business has a massive educational job to do. Perhaps as a start it might throw away a lot of the old inspirational literature on selling and let the facts of the new situation do the inspiring.[3]

And, according to a feature article in *The Wall Street Journal,*[4] the steel companies—driven by the threat of increasing idle capacity— are departing from past practice by recognizing and implementing the new approach.

A Common Cause

When the concept of customer orientation and the accompanying planning process are fully, continually, and consistently implemented, they have a beneficial impact on every job from the top to the bottom of the business. They bring the organization chart to life. Even more important, they permit individuals to conceive of their jobs in much more meaningful terms than are expressed by any organization chart. They describe the business as what it is and what it expects to become. Thus they establish a common cause for all the individuals in the business and any others who may join it.

These terms identify the nature and extent of the specific individual contributions to be made to the common cause. Standards of

[2] From a talk, "New Potentials in Salesmanship," before the Thirty-third Annual Boston Conference on Distribution, 1961.
[3] "The Salesman Isn't Dead—He's Different," *Fortune,* November 1962, p. 124.
[4] January 16, 1963.

performance thereby are established which are not determined in abstract but are developed by the people involved and are formalized on the basis of mutual understanding as to what is possible under all the circumstances, both external and internal to the business. Such standards are directly related to the profitable growth of the business and so provide a true incentive for men seeking security of opportunity. They can and must be used, first of all, in self-measurement of progress.

These terms identify the critical interrelationships of individual jobs throughout the business. They provide the understanding and incentive so necessary for teamwork rather than internecine warfare. Not only do they assure better understanding of individual jobs and better evaluation of performance, but they also permit the building of more responsibility and authority into each job. Management at all levels can delegate without abdicating. More management content can be included in more positions throughout the business. Within limits understandable to the individual, each can become more the master of his own destiny in his job.

Customer-oriented planning further provides a foundation upon which an effective communication system can be established—and the problem of communication is becoming more acute daily, for small as well as big businesses. Individuals at all levels and locations are hampered and frustrated in their activities by the lack of current, complete information on matters of importance and by the deluge of unimportant information. They spend endless hours in conference and on paperwork in an effort to keep informed. Not only is much of this time and effort wasted, but it detracts from other, more creative work.

One of the more popular pastimes in business circles recently has been to recognize this problem by establishing elaborate studies and, eventually, procedures directed at streamlining communication per se. If these studies and procedures are undertaken without the proper focus, they not only are doomed to failure from the beginning but are very likely to lead to a streamlining of the wrong kind of information. The cure, in other words, may turn out to be worse than the disease. The proper focus is provided by the answers to the basic questions: What information is necessary, and who must have it for sound planning? All the various pieces of the communication system for planning and controlling the business will fall into place around these answers. Without them, a monster may be born, beloved of its creators but bemoaned by others in the business who are burdened by authorized and formalized (rather than informal) confusion.

The Process Applied Personally

Every man owes himself the opportunity to develop and express himself to the limit of his potential. He should take a reading on his score from time to time. Otherwise he may wake up some day to find that he either has missed his opportunities altogether or is not measuring up to the ones facing him. This is tragic for the individual and harmful to the business with which he is associated.

In the same way that a business can analyze what it is and what it can expect to become by following this approach, so an individual can take a reading on himself and his current and future place in the business. That is, with a few paraphrases the business planning process can be applied personally. Each individual in business has his own situation. What is the need of the business that he is trying to serve? What are its performance, appearance, economic, and service requirements? Who are his direct and indirect customers within the business? What is his direct and indirect competition? What capability does he have and what more is required to serve this need profitably for himself and the business? What, specifically, is his chosen area of operation? His purpose? If a man can answer these questions to his satisfaction and will remind himself of them from time to time, he should be much better equipped to recognize his best opportunities in the business and to establish and follow through with strategies, objectives, and targets for his and the company's mutual benefit.

When the individual is associated with the right business, what is good for the individual should be good for the business. Sound planning on the part of business and of the individual is necessary if security of opportunity is to be achieved by both.

The suggestions in this book should result in what might be called a system for business operation which will step back and let the individual take over—as every good system should. No method, technique, or system can replace man. At best, it can only assist man to realize his dreams for himself and others. This system should breed, rather than impede, the innovator and the bold.

INDEX

Index

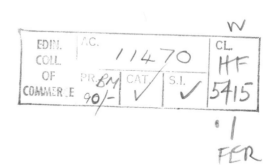

About the Author

Robert W. Ferrell, Director of Marketing Development at Owens–Illinois, has had wide experience in both the formulation and the application of market-oriented planning techniques. At General Electric Company he first served as a general corporate attorney and legal counsel, and was then appointed Manager–Employee and Community Relations. After several managerial assignments he helped to organize the Marketing Service operation, and he was especially concerned with the explanation and installation of the marketing concept in all the operating departments of GE.

At Owens–Illinois Mr. Ferrell is responsible for developing marketing techniques and advising their application to the operating divisions. He also directs the practice of marketing with respect to corporate matters and the evaluation of operating division marketing activities.

Mr. Ferrell is a graduate of the University of Richmond and the Harvard Law School, and he attended the Harvard Business School's Advanced Management Course. For GE, he co-authored *Marketing Organization Guide* and *An Approach to Marketing Planning*, which was the company's first formal statement concerning planning techniques.